"This fascinating, first-hand account of the clash between an Amazonian frontier proletariat and a global oil-extraction industry teaches us more about the conditions of global capitalism than any abstract theory could provide. A wonderfully written account of what it is like to join an uprising when solidarity comes from the justice of the struggle, and the Indigenous is not the other, but yourself. This is theory at its concrete best."

Susan Buck-Morss, *Cornell University and CUNY Graduate Center, USA*

"Against the decolonial rejection of universalism, this book is an elegant and brilliant personal account of insurgent universality in the Ecuadorian Amazon, in which Indigenous peoples and other subalterns join ranks against multinational capital based not on cultural or racial identity but shared experiences of alienation and dispossession, united in concrete struggles of universality from below. An absolute must-read for anyone interested in questions of subaltern rebellion and solidarity today."

Ilan Kapoor, *York University, Canada*

"In this timely book, Japhy Wilson unearths the lived reality of a subaltern struggle on the extractive frontier of the Ecuadorian Amazon that challenges the cultural relativism of today's progressive academic establishment. Arguing that the aim of the struggle was not to defend Indigenous identities, but to reclaim dignity, equality, and better living conditions, the book makes a compelling case for 'the actuality of universal humanity,' and offers a vivid glimpse of real plebeian politics."

Martín Arboleda, *Universidad Diego Portales, Chile*

"Reporting from an uprising of workers and communities in the Ecuadorian Amazon, *Extractivism and Universality* combines rich empirical research with deft theoretical exposition. Departing from standard academic narratives, Japhy Wilson invites the reader to grasp the political practices and collective struggles that point beyond the stale binary between Eurocentric universalism and an Indigenous pluriverse."

Thomas F Purcell, *King's College London, UK*

Extractivism and Universality

What are the possibilities for a radical politics of universal humanity, at a time when the politics of identity increasingly defines the agenda of the left? What are the political and conceptual implications of such an emancipatory form of universality emerging through the struggles of Indigenous peoples on the extractive frontiers of global capitalism? How do such battles play out on the ground, and how should they be researched and conveyed?

Extractivism and Universality takes an unorthodox approach to these timely questions. It tells the inside story of a spontaneous uprising in the Ecuadorian Amazon in 2017, in which mestizo, Black, and Indigenous workers and communities confronted the combined forces of a multinational oil company and a militarized state. The book documents a rapidly evolving battle that achieved a remarkable victory and captures the flourishing of an insurgent form of political universality in which racial, ethnic, and cultural divisions were suddenly and powerfully overcome. Intervening in debates on the resistances and alternatives developed by the inhabitants of resource extraction zones, it takes the reader deep inside a rebellion on an Amazonian oil frontier and offers a unique insight into insurgent universality in the lived reality of its material existence. It argues that the dominant decolonial dichotomy between Eurocentric universalism and an Indigenous pluriverse should be replaced by an approach that is attentive to manifestations of universality performed by diverse subaltern subjects. And it does so through a fast-paced fusion of radical political theory with the raw first-person style of gonzo journalism. It will appeal to scholars and students across the social sciences with interests in political and social theory, social movements, labor relations, and the political ecology of extractivism.

Japhy Wilson is Honorary Research Fellow in Politics at the University of Manchester. His research explores the politics of development and the possibilities of radical transformation under conditions of global capitalism. He is the author of *Reality of Dreams: Post-Neoliberal Utopias in the Ecuadorian Amazon* (Yale University Press) and *Jeffrey Sachs: The Strange Case of Dr. Shock and Mr. Aid* (Verso), and co-editor of *The Post-Political and Its Discontents: Spaces of Depoliticization, Spectres of Radical Politics* (Edinburgh University Press).

Critiques and Alternatives to Capitalism
Series editor: Marcello Musto, Professor of Sociological Theory, York University, Canada

This series publishes scholarly works on critiques and alternatives to capitalism, spanning a number of subject matters, political perspectives and geographical areas. It welcomes monographs and edited volumes in the fields of sociology, social and political theory and heterodox political economy, whose main areas of focus are the problems of capitalist society and its mode of production; alternatives to capitalism that address contemporary social issues; and 19th and 20th centuries anti-capitalist ideas and practical experiments.

Welcoming new perspectives on a wide range of themes, it seeks to explore alternative social-economic systems, critical theories of capitalism, social classes and inequality, public/private ownership and new contours of 'the commons', economic and financial crises, ecology, globalization, migration and citizenship, gender oppression, alienation, and cultural critique. The result is an eclectic, but focused and informative, series that provides original investigations, inspires significant conversations for today, and appeals to a diverse international audience.

For more information about this series, please visit:
https://www.routledge.com/Critiques-and-Alternatives-to-Capitalism/book-series/CAATC

Titles in this series

Extractivism and Universality
Inside an Uprising in the Amazon
Japhy Wilson

A Critical Theory of Economic Compulsion
Wealth, Suffering, Negation
Werner Bonefeld

Alternative Futures and the Present
Postcolonial Possibilities
Ranabir Samaddar

Extractivism and Universality

Inside an Uprising in the Amazon

Japhy Wilson

Routledge
Taylor & Francis Group
LONDON AND NEW YORK

First published 2023
by Routledge
2 Park Square, Milton Park, Abingdon, Oxon OX14 4RN

and by Routledge
605 Third Avenue, New York, NY 10158

Routledge is an imprint of the Taylor & Francis Group, an informa business

British Library Cataloguing-in-Publication Data
A catalogue record for this book is available from the British Library

ISBN: 9781032386126 (hbk)
ISBN: 9781032386164 (pbk)
ISBN: 9781003345879 (ebk)

DOI: 10.4324/9781003345879

Typeset in Times New Roman
by Deanta Global Publishing Services, Chennai, India

Dedicated to the motley crew of the Savage Road

Contents

Acknowledgments

I stumbled into the uprising that this book depicts. And by the time I was smuggled out of there nine days later, concealed from the cops in the back of a truck before dawn, I knew I had to tell the story. But a gonzo account of an anonymous struggle on an obscure resource frontier was always going to be something of a long shot in the uptight market-focused world of academic publishing. And all the more so, given that the story challenges certain cherished shibboleths of today's critical scholarly elite, in its affirmation of universal humanity against the politics of racial, ethnic, and cultural particularism, and in its depiction of Indigenous peoples fighting alongside mestizo settlers for their rights as workers in the oil industry, instead of opposing extractivism in the name of ecological purity and cultural tradition. The hegemony of this elite, and its capacity to blacklist authors and publishers who are perceived to have violated its ideological axioms, caused this book's publication to be blocked on more than one occasion. Amazingly enough, one editor refused to take the manuscript to his editorial board, even though the book was already under contract, and even after the two reviews he had commissioned had both unambiguously recommended its publication. In his words:

> It's frustrating for me (and I suspect you) to be in a position where it's hard to move ahead despite supportive reports ... And while I don't want to avoid challenging, heterodox material, I'm just not confident in my own ability to shepherd this sort of thing through the board approval process.

In another case, the book was rejected after one potential reviewer declined to review the manuscript, as they considered it to be "hostile to decolonial studies, Indigenous studies, gender studies, and most of the fields I care a great deal about." I will leave it to the reader to decide if this is an accurate description of a book that celebrates the struggles of Indigenous peoples in general, and of Indigenous women in particular. Perhaps what this non-reviewer really objected to was the book's disruption of the boundaries of these fields of study, which are heavily policed in the increasingly paranoid defense of a peculiarly colonial fantasy that predetermines what subaltern subjects care about and how they behave.

At any rate, the trials and tribulations of this book's journey to publication mean that I am profoundly grateful to all those who have helped to get it into print.

Thanks first and foremost to Marcello Musto, editor of the anti-capitalist series of which I am honored that the book is now a part, who has renewed my faith in the enduring possibility of comradeship in the increasingly careerist context of neoliberal academia. The book's existence is also due to the equally comradely interventions of Mazen Labban, who fully supported the project from the start, and those of Martín Arboleda, whose enthusiasm helped to convince me of its viability when I first pitched the idea to him and Mazen, several beers into an intense discussion in the inappropriately genteel setting of a Harvard bar. Both Mazen and Martín offered incisive comments on early drafts, which immensely strengthened the text. Tom Purcell's generous and keenly observed review was also crucial in convincing me to get rid of what needed to be cut. I received further invaluable feedback and insights from Erik Swyngedouw, Ioanna Tantanasi, Estefanía Martínez, Sofía Jarrín, Gerard Coffey, Kai Heron, Ilan Kapoor, Bjørn Enge Bertelsen and Salvatore Engel-Di Mauro. I am immensely grateful to Natalia Valdivieso for conducting some last-minute field research on my behalf, which enabled me to tie up some vital loose ends. I would also like to thank my brother Owen, who gave me an anthology of Hunter S. Thompson's gonzo journalism several years ago as an antidote to the desiccated abstraction of conventional academic writing – thank you for inspiring the style of this book! And thanks to Neil Jordan at Routledge for his willingness to pursue this unconventional project, and to Gemma Rogers for her sound editorial advice.

Things would never have got this far without Ioanna, who made sure the audio files with which I documented the uprising were safely dispatched from Ecuador under threat of police seizure, and who has put up with my bullshit before and since – as lover, as reader, and now as mother to our little rebel Molly Thank you for sticking by me through thick and thin.

My greatest thanks go to those involved in the uprising itself. For welcoming me into their fight. For saving my skin on more than one occasion. And for teaching me a powerful lesson about the ineradicable actuality of the insurgent universal, which this book does its best to convey. In particular, the street fighters whose names – or pseudonyms – fill the story, and whose words and actions set it alight: Luis Barberan, Jimmy Chamba, Edison Kapáku, Rosa Kapáku, Marco Kapáku, Linda Kapáku, Bolívar Naichap, Olger Naichap, Pedro, Tigrillo, Santiago Jempekta, Darío Rodríguez, Manuel Méndez, and Juan Santiak. *Viva el paro!*

1 We Are All Indigenous

The spear came to a sudden stop, right between his eyes. It had been thrust out of the crowd that filled the doorway. Its point had been sharpened with shards of broken glass found on the roadside, during days and nights standing watch against a long-anticipated military crackdown. Now it came to rest, ever so gently, on the forehead of the fake cop. "Give him back his passport," said the Indigenous leader of the renegades surrounding the door. The fake cop put my passport in my hand. I stepped out into the sunlight and the crowd closed around me. Together we walked back down the Savage Road, toward the gates of the oil company and the site of the blockade.

The Savage Road – the *Vía Auca.* That's what it had always been called, ever since it was sliced into the Ecuadorian Amazon back in 1979. It was named after the "*aucas*" – or savages – as they were disparagingly known: the *Huaorani* Indigenous nationality who inhabited the south bank of the Napo River. The road ran deep into their territory, following the path of newly discovered oil wells. Its true savagery was not that of the people it dispossessed, but of the industry it sustained. A tangle of pipelines stretched beside it, along with pumping stations, worker camps, rough towns, gas flares, waste pits, and oil spills. Just another savage road on the Amazon frontier.

Like most extractive frontiers, the Savage Road had seen its share of boom and bust. And right now, things were booming once again. In 2015, the Ecuadorian state had signed a multi-billion-dollar deal with Schlumberger – a Franco-American multinational and the largest oilfield services company in the world – for the exploitation of Block 61, otherwise known as the Auca field. Block 61 was one of the richest fields in the Ecuadorian oil industry, and all the oil it produced was pumped out along the *Vía Auca.* Now Schlumberger was rapidly ramping up production, based on the drilling of dozens of new wells. This implied a vast infrastructural expansion involving the construction of new platforms, roads, and pipelines. A production complex employing over 1,000 workers had been built for this purpose on the outskirts of Dayuma – the biggest town on the Savage Road, with work beginning in January 2016.

I arrived in Dayuma in August 2017. I was hoping to speak to the settlers who had first colonized the region, as part of my research on the recent history of the Ecuadorian Amazon.[1] But as I passed the gates of the production complex, I could

DOI: 10.4324/9781003345879-1

see a demonstration taking place outside. And within hours of my arrival, I found myself caught up in the midst of a labor dispute, which quickly escalated into a more serious and generalized conflict, involving the detention of the strike organizers, the kidnapping of the construction company manager, the blockading of the production complex, the launch of a military operation to break the blockade, the revelation of a plot to assassinate the leaders of the uprising, and the unleashing of a fluid and rapidly evolving battle against seemingly impossible odds that was destined to achieve a remarkable victory.

This book tells the inside story of this struggle. It provides a real-time account on an otherwise unreported uprising on an Amazonian oil frontier, which aims to capture the cut and thrust of a revolt led by rebellious workers against the combined might of multinational capital and the nation state, as one of countless struggles that occur in similar conditions in equally remote places, but that remain invisible to the rest of the world. It traces the twists and turns of a dangerous and chaotic process, documenting its repeated disruption by unforeseen events and drawing out its traversal by a steadily ascending arc of radicalization and political subjectivation. This story is narrated from the perspective of someone immersed within it, with all the bewilderment and adrenaline that this entails.

In this sense, the book is a concentrated blast of political reportage, which has been researched and written in the spirit of the gonzo journalism pioneered by Hunter S. Thompson. Gonzo rejects the mainstream journalistic pretense of objectivity as "a pompous contradiction in terms," and places the journalist at the center of the action, based on the principle that "the writer must be a participant in the scene."[2] Though best known for his personal documentation of dystopian decadence in *Fear and Loathing in Las Vegas*, Thompson's early gonzo experiments were politically charged works that reported on his direct involvement with radical social movements and rebel biker gangs, through which he sought to gain a deeper insight into these renegade collectives than was possible from the perspective of the supposedly objective external observer.[3]

Having been unexpectedly pitched into the maelstrom this book depicts, I soon decided to abandon the more conventional research project that had brought me to the region, and to remain in the thick of this wildly spiraling confrontation, drawing on my memories of Thompson's texts as a methodological inspiration. Gonzo, however, is about form as well as method. The challenge lies not only in full involvement in the events that are to be reported, but also in communicating this experience in a direct and unmediated way.[4] To this end, Thompson wrote in raw prose from a first-person perspective, basing his texts directly on his notes and transcripts, and maintaining a frenetic pace throughout. The resulting style has been described as "a literary Molotov cocktail."[5] Or as Thompson himself put it:

> The basic concept … was to lash the whole thing together and essentially record the reality of an incredibly volatile [event] as it was happening. *From an eye in the eye of the hurricane*, as it were … What I would like to preserve is a kind of high-speed cinematic reel-record of what [the situation] was like at the time, not what the whole thing boils down to or how it fits into history.[6]

I have followed Thompson's lead in this regard, by setting out to write what he would call a "nonfiction novel."[7] The period of my own involvement in the uprising is reported in the first person and the present tense; the actions and events are described in a style that aims to remain as close to the bone as possible; and the narrative contains no conceptual summaries or theoretical reflections, apart from those hinted at in my fieldnotes themselves. Unlike Thompson, however, I am not a journalist but an academic, and I cannot help considering what the uprising "boils down to" and "how it fits into history." This, in fact, is the central purpose of the story I am about to tell, beyond providing a "high-speed cinematic reel-record" of the struggle itself. The remainder of this introductory chapter sketches some preliminary ideas about such matters, which breathe through the subsequent narration of events, before being revisited and further developed in the final chapter of the book. I keep it short and to the point. Then we plunge into the hurricane.

*****

This book is a personal account of a particular event. But it also bears witness to the fleeting emergence of an insurgent form of political universality. This is not an uncontroversial claim. Universalism is something of a dirty word in critical scholarship these days, and the erstwhile project of universal emancipation now tends to be regarded as complicit with a colonial commitment to replacing multiple realities with a single Western world. Many scholars committed to the project of decolonization have rightly noted the role that universalism has played in providing the colonial project with a veneer of moral sanctity and scientific objectivity. They have identified the tendency for dogmatic strains of Marxist universalism to conceal the interests of white male factory workers in the Global North beneath a discourse of universal proletarian struggle, and to reproduce the colonial narrative of inevitable historical progress toward a distinctly Western modernity. And they have documented the repeated imposition of a civilizing mission on peasants and Indigenous peoples through the Marxist–Leninist doctrine of an urban intellectual vanguard.[8]

From this perspective, universalism is a "bimillennial patriarchal, repressive, transcendent, racist and phallocratic narrative that runs like a red thread throughout the West's history, from Saint Paul to Marx … and beyond."[9] The decolonial rejection of universalism has contributed to the recent emergence of a radical political and theoretical project in opposition to capitalist development in general and to development based on natural resource extraction – or extractivism – in particular.[10] The decolonial critique of extractivism rejects universalism in both its colonial and orthodox Marxist versions as a top-down imposition, and seeks to replace it with a "pluriverse" in which diverse Indigenous cultures can coexist and flourish in their differentiated lifeworlds.[11] The pluriverse has been defined as "a broad transcultural compilation of concrete concepts, worldviews and practices from around the world, challenging the modernist ontology of universalism in favor of a multiplicity of possible worlds."[12] This vision is grounded in the practices and experiences of the subaltern subjects of the Global South – particularly those of Indigenous and Afro-descendant peoples, and demands a shift from conceiving "politics as power relations within a singular world," to including "the possibility of adversarial relations among worlds."[13] In contexts such as the uprising in which I was involved, a decolonial approach would begin from

> these "other" perspectives and their marking and construction of a different critical thought that is not singular but plural in formation, and that finds base and reason not in modernity but in the histories, subjectivities, and knowledges that coloniality has marked.[14]

But what if such an approach were to result, not in the revelation of a pluriverse, but in a glimpse of an alternative universality? I was thrown without warning into the uprising on the Savage Road, and my interpretation of the situation was largely reliant on the perspectives of the subaltern subjects involved in the struggle, and the critical thought that they were formulating – precisely the approach advocated by decolonial theory. But I soon began to sense a universal spirit in the air, which was not being imposed on a pluriverse of Indigenous identities but was being enacted through Indigenous identity itself. The uprising included a complex mixture of races and ethnicities: mestizos, Afro-descendants, members of the *Shuar*, *Kichwa*, and *Huaorani* Indigenous nationalities, and my own identity as a white Anglo-American male. Addressing this diverse and impassioned crowd on the morning of the third day of the uprising, a *Shuar* leader called on all men present to strip to the waist, and told everyone to seize spears and paint their faces in the symbolic red juice of the *achiote* seed: "We are going to paint ourselves," he declared, "because we are all Indigenous!"

This was not the first time in the course of the struggle that such a message had been articulated, but it was only now that I began to sense its significance. My fieldnotes from that day record my initial reflections on his words as follows:

> By noon the sun is intolerable, and everyone takes shelter beneath the makeshift black plastic marquee … I find myself a space between others sitting and lying on the oil pipes that run between the road and the houses. A few general notes while I am sitting here … Everyone stripping off their shirts and taking up spears was an affirmation of unity-in-difference. Not "we are all mestizos," [as one might expect from the critical literature equating universality with the colonial erasure of Indigenous identity,] but "*we are all Indigenous*."

The uprising, I rather clumsily concluded, "is an amazing fusion of cultures and ethnicities in which everyone is united against the company."

My inarticulate sense of a counterintuitive form of universality emerging spontaneously within the uprising intensified as the struggle continued. This was not a dry universalism drawn from dogmatic manifestos, but a living universality that leapt from the flames of a sudden confrontation. Not a working class of white men defending their privileged position in the stable core of the global system, but a ragtag gang of women and men, Black and white, Indigenous and mestizo, fighting tooth and nail on the extractive frontier. Not the steady march of historical progress toward a universal future, but a moment of temporal rupture in which universality was immediately present. And not the imported ideology of foreign intellectuals, but the boisterous self-expression of unschooled renegades.

It was only later that I found a way of framing this experience in theoretical terms. The key lay in the pages of *Hegel, Haiti, and Universal History*, in which Susan Buck-Morss challenges the contemporary dismissal of universality in critical scholarship, arguing that "the project of universal freedom does not need to be discarded but, rather, redeemed and reconstituted on a different basis."[15] Her argument is based, not on theoretical abstractions, but on the concrete history of the Haitian Revolution of 1791–1804, in which the Black slaves of Saint-Domingue overthrew their colonial masters and founded the Haitian state. The slaves revealed the hypocrisy of the French Revolution, which framed itself in the language of universal freedom, but which failed to extend this principle to the enslaved populations of its colonies. But they did so not in defense of their race or ethnicity but in the name of universality itself. Field slaves and free laborers were united in rebellion, and racial hierarchies were eradicated from the new constitution of the Haitian state, in which all Haitians were defined as Black regardless of their race.[16]

Buck-Morss also draws attention to Peter Linebaugh and Marcus Rediker's radical history of Atlantic commerce, which describes the extent to which the English colonial expansion of the seventeenth and eighteenth centuries was both enabled and subverted by the unruly labor of Indigenous peoples, "dispossessed commoners, transported felons, indentured servants … and African slaves." This "motley crew" led strikes, riots, and mutinies, creating autonomous maroon communities in remote jungles and on uninhabited islands, and running pirate ships on egalitarian principles, according to which rank was abolished, and spoils were enjoyed in common.[17] Together they comprised a frontier proletariat, understood not as a reductive homogenizing abstraction, but as what Alain Badiou would call "a particularly multifaceted non-totalizable ensemble."[18] This frontier proletariat was formed by the most marginalized and outcast elements of multiple nations, cultures, and walks of life. Yet precisely for this reason, Buck-Morss suggests, its collective actions gave expression to a "universalism from below."[19]

These examples lead Buck-Morss to reformulate universality in terms that decolonize the concept, while simultaneously disrupting the politics of identity expressed in the anti-universalist concept of the pluriverse:

> The definition of universal history that begins to emerge here is this: rather than giving multiple, distinct cultures equal due, whereby people are recognized as part of humanity indirectly through the mediation of collective cultural identities, human universality emerges in the historical event at the point of rupture. It is in the discontinuities of history that people whose cultures have been strained to breaking point give expression to a humanity that goes beyond cultural limits. And it is in our empathic identification with this

raw, free and vulnerable state, that we have a chance of understanding what they say. Common humanity exists in spite of culture and its differences.[20]

This form of universality has been defined by Massimiliano Tomba as an "insurgent universality," which is "constituted by individuals who act in common and put in question the hierarchical organization of the social fabric."[21] Insurgent universality is not the legacy of colonial Europe, but of the victims of its oppression, and arises not from the abstract doctrines of Western intellectuals, but from the concrete struggles of the oppressed peoples of the Global South. Such struggles are opposed to the false universalisms of state and capital. As Slavoj Žižek argues, "We are dealing here with two opposed logics of universality to be strictly distinguished ... Not only are the two not the same, but the struggle is ultimately ... a struggle between [these] two exclusive forms of universality themselves."[22]

The affirmation of insurgent universality is consistent with decolonial theory, both in its rejection of top-down universalism and to the extent that it builds theory on the basis of subaltern battles, rather than imposing it on these battles from outside. Indeed, it resonates with the anti-Eurocentric universality of one of the great inspirations for the decolonial project, Frantz Fanon. For Fanon, universal humanity is "something which Europe has been incapable of achieving," and can only be realized by those peoples on whose exclusion and exploitation the colonial project has been constructed.[23] But the dichotomy that decolonial critique has tended to establish between top-down universalism and a bottom-up pluriverse threatens to blind it to manifestations of insurgent universality performed by subaltern subjects in their confrontations with extractive capital.[24] Instead, as Buck-Morss insists, we need to be attentive to the possibility that "universal humanity is visible at the edges," while seeking to grasp the universal "not by subsuming facts within overarching systems or homogenizing premises, but by attending to the edges of systems."[25]

Buck-Morss's exploration of such edges is based on her analysis of historical events. But how can such a phenomenon be grasped as it emerges in the present? This returns us to Hunter S. Thompson, who refers to his gonzo methodology as "edgework," in which the researcher joins their subversive research subjects in violating the limits set by social norms and legal order.[26] Edgework has inspired a radical strain of criminology known as "edge ethnography,"[27] which holds that a true understanding of the nature of crime demands that the criminologist "must share, to whatever extent possible, in the dangers, pleasures, emotions and experiences that constitute criminal activity."[28] I would argue that the same is the case for spontaneous uprisings such as the one in which I was involved. Not only because such events are often criminalized – as occurred in this case – but more importantly because their transgression of the established order releases collective energies that can only be fully experienced by those who cross the line.

A similar point has been made by Alain Badiou, who frames the global present as a time of "riots and uprisings," which he depicts as moments of "intensive super-existence" that transcend the differences between those involved.[29] Reflecting on his own involvement in such events, Badiou claims that

> a new political situation can only be known from within its own process, and that ordinary news and commentary are not enough. And there is a very simple reason for that: political novelty, which is subjective, does not allow itself to be grasped from the outside at the moment of constituting itself.[30]

This is the essence of edgework, which is likewise based on full immersion in the intense events it documents, as the only means of accessing their inner truth. Gonzo, in other words, turns out to be a good method for grasping the insurgent universal as it emerges "at the moment of constituting itself" – and this is so precisely because of its insistence on the primacy of the particular and the subjective. To this end, I have not edited myself out of the story told in this book, as is so often the case in academic writing. Instead, I have sought to reproduce events as they played out through my eyes, infused with my own enthusiasm and anxiety, in order to better convey the lived reality of the uprising and the sense of universality that emerged within it, which was simultaneously subjective and collective.

*****

And that's enough of that. Any more theorizing at this stage would be in danger of seriously missing the point, by beginning to erect an abstract conceptual edifice of precisely the kind that insurgent universality destabilizes and subverts. Or as Hunter S. Thompson would say: "This gibberish could run on for ever and ever … The time has come to get full bore into heavy Gonzo Journalism, and this time we have no choice but to push it all the way out to the limit."[31]

2 The Savage Road

The Savage Road cuts into the jungle in a straight line, north to south. Like a knife into the stomach, plunged in and driven sharply down. It runs for 60 miles or so from the town of Coca, which stands on the north bank of the Napo River. A rapacious gang of conquistadors came through here in 1541 on the way to "discovering" the Amazon River, and capital has been tearing into the Amazon Basin ever since, gorging itself on hardwoods, hydrocarbons, minerals, medicinal plants, wild rubber, and agricultural land. The Ecuadorian Amazon didn't see much of this action for the first four centuries or so. It was hundreds of miles upriver from the Brazilian and Peruvian extractive frontiers to the east, and the Andes stood between it and the impoverished Ecuadorian state to the west. But in 1967, oil was discovered here. Within a few years, a highway and a pipeline had been run over the mountains to the Pacific coast, and the Ecuadorian Amazon had become a new frontier of global capitalism, as the epicenter of an oil boom.[1]

Texaco held the first concession, which they operated in partnership with the Ecuadorian state. They first struck oil near the Colombian border. Further strikes led them in the direction of Coca, before crossing the Napo and continuing into the unexplored jungles that lay on the other side. For most Ecuadorians, this region was known only as a land of "beasts and savages" (*fieras y aucas*). The supposed savages in question were the *Huaorani* – nomadic hunter-gatherers who were feared and despised in equal measure. The *Huaorani* had arrived in the region in the early twentieth century, escaping genocidal slave-hunting missions launched by Peruvian rubber traders backed by European capital. Their territory now stretched from the south bank of the Napo along the full length of the future road. When they needed to defend it, they did so by any means necessary. In the 1930s, they became notorious among mestizo settlers and urban Ecuadorians for murdering loggers and rubber tappers who strayed into their land. In 1956, five American missionaries attempted to establish contact with them and were killed. A more successful contact was made two years later, and the *Huaorani* were gradually assimilated and resettled. But two splinter groups – the *Tagaeri* and the *Taromenane* – remained in "voluntary isolation" and continued to violently oppose all those who threatened their territory.[2]

The oil workers were dropped by helicopter into this fearsome situation. They set up crude camps, from which chainsaw gangs hacked their way into the jungle,

DOI: 10.4324/9781003345879-2

clearing paths for seismic tests – dynamite explosions that shook the earth to show where oil lay. The first strike on this side of the Napo came in 1970, and the invasion of *Huaorani* territory by state and capital immediately intensified. The following year saw the first counterattacks by the *Tagaeri* – wounding two oil workers and killing a cook who had been left alone in camp. But oil had been found, and exploration proceeded apace, pushing further south into the territory of the so-called *aucas*.

The *Huaorani* soon began visiting the camps. Before long, many were working for the oil companies, and blowing their wages in the nearest bars and brothels.[3] Meanwhile, the *Tagaeri* and *Taromenane* continued to resist in the face of repeated displacements, the progressive depletion of their hunting grounds, and the murder with impunity of their members by oil workers, illegal loggers, and the military. In 1976, two crossed *Tagaeri* spears were found blocking the path of a seismic grid cut through the jungle. The company refused to heed the warning and forced the explorations to continue. Three workers were murdered by the *Tagaeri* six months later. The discovery of their bodies was described by a member of the rescue team:

> We found Mr. Paredes first, facedown, with three spears through his back. Further into the jungle we found Mr. Guarnizo, who had been run through by five spears. They had attacked him face on, and his eyes were bulging out of his head in horror … Further on, behind a tree trunk where he had tried to hide himself, we found Mr. Rivera with seven spears buried in his body. One of them had gone straight through his head. Those *aucas* were merciless with those three men.[4]

In the words of a foreman stationed in the region at the time:

> Oil has no rules for this kind of thing. It thinks of nothing, not the lives of the workers, nor those of the *Huaorani* and *Tagaeri*. The oil must be extracted from the bowels of the earth, regardless of where it happens to be found.[5]

Following the deaths of these workers, the exploration of the region swiftly resumed. By this time, Ecuador had been transformed from a semi-feudal agricultural economy into a modern oil nation, which was highly dependent on Amazonian oil revenues for the development of its metropolitan regions in the highlands and on the coast. The first oilfields were already reaching maturity, and extensive new reserves had now been found south of the Napo. A bridge was built across the river from Coca, and the construction of a road began in 1979.[6] Everyone called it "the Savage Road."

*****

The *Vía Auca* opened a new frontier of spontaneous colonization. Ever since the first highway had arrived in the Amazon from the capital city of Quito a decade earlier, landless peasants had been flooding in and settling along the oil roads. This process was encouraged by the government, which saw it as a means of avoiding social conflict without the redistribution of land and power in other parts of the country. Ignoring the Indigenous population of the region, a law designated the northern Amazon as *tierras baldias* – vacant lands. Anyone willing to settle the region could claim a *finca* – a 124-acre parcel measuring 800 by 6,600 feet with the narrow side facing the road. Another row of plots would then be cut behind the first, and so on, deep into the jungle. The settlers – or *colonos* as they were known – would show up and stake their claim, clearing the jungle with machetes, defending their land with shotguns, and dealing with the paperwork later. The physical presence of the state was limited to the roads themselves, and the military camps set up to defend the oil wells.[7]

The Savage Road lay at the most desolate and dangerous perimeter of this unbridled frontier. It was the kind of place that attracted those with nothing left to lose. Impoverished mestizo peasants arrived here in the early 1980s from the drought-stricken state of Loja in the highlands and founded precarious settlements with utopian names like *La Belleza* (Beauty) and hard-bitten names like *El Esfuerzo* (The Striving). They were joined by marginalized members of historical maroon communities created during the colonial period by escaped African slaves on the Ecuadorian coast,[8] who established a small Black settlement on the *Vía Auca* called *Ciudad Blanca* (White City). Indigenous *comunas* were also created here, using legal statutes that had been developed for highland Indigenous communities to defend their territorial claims.[9] Some were formed by members of the *Kichwa* nationality, who had recently escaped from a system of indentured slavery that had persisted along the banks of the Napo since the time of the rubber boom. Others were created by members of the *Shuar*, some of whom had been expelled from their original communities in the southern Amazon and were rumored to be running from the law. And then, there were undocumented Colombian conmen who acquired large tracts of land in dubious ways, prostitutes working the brothels along the roadside, and timber smugglers paying the army to look the other way.[10]

This motley crew also included members of the *Huaorani*, who had abandoned the forest and established communities at the far end of the road, and thousands of oil workers housed in multiple oil camps.[11] By the mid-1980s, the *Vía Auca* had become the focal point of the Ecuadorian oil frontier. The Auca field was producing 50,000 barrels a day, and new blocks were being sold off to foreign capital.[12] Meanwhile, the *colonos* were doing pretty well – land was plentiful, soils were fertile, coffee and cattle prices were high, and there was plenty of temporary work in the oil industry. In the words of Pablo Gallegos, a liberation theologian and Carmelite missionary based in the region: "It was like a paradise. They had fish. They had wild animals. Whatever they planted flourished. So it was marvelous for them. Everything was new. Everything was virgin."[13]

It didn't stay that way for long. In 1987, two Capuchin missionaries attempted to establish contact with a group of *Tagaeri*, in the hope of avoiding another bloody confrontation with the oil workers who continued to encroach upon their territory. They were murdered on arrival.[14] For those who had colonized the region, it was a harbinger of more difficult times to come. Soon the bottom had dropped out of the coffee market, and yields were collapsing as the initial fertility of the thin soils was exhausted. And now there was no more land left to colonize. The *fincas* had reached the limits of the Yasuni National Park, which had been established at the time of the construction of the *Vía Auca*. The park overlapped with the *Zona Intangible* (Intangible Zone), which had been created in the aftermath of the murder of the Capuchin missionaries as a reserve for the *Tagaeri* and *Taromenane*. The *Huaorani* had also been granted a significant extension of territory, and *Kichwa* and *Shuar comunas* occupied the rest of the land. In this context, the trafficking of land accelerated, and violent conflicts intensified between competing groups.[15]

Meanwhile in the oil industry, the exploration and construction phase had almost concluded. Once the oil was flowing, only a handful of security guards and engineers were required to keep the system running. Unemployment spiraled, the worker camps emptied, and demand for local goods and services evaporated. The settlements that had sprung up along the Savage Road were also confronting a chronic lack of water, electricity, and sanitation, and a near-total absence of schools and medical care. The road itself was a death trap – potholed and surfaced with stones, punctuated by single-lane bridges, and traveled at dangerous speeds by supply trucks and oil tankers. The companies covered it in waste oil to keep down the dust, and the rains drained the oil into the streams and rivers. Oil leaked from decrepit pipelines, fumes billowed from grimy gas flares, and millions of gallons of highly toxic formation waters were flushed straight into the jungle.[16] Pits of waste oil would sporadically catch fire, raging for days and filling the skies with ash that fell back to earth as "black rain." Before long, cancers were proliferating in this "rainforest Chernobyl."[17] The depth of the crisis is conveyed by the following extracts from a locally produced environmental report on the *Vía Auca*:

> An oil spill has contaminated the vegetation of a *finca* called *El Futuro* (The Future) … no clean-up has been conducted; oil spills have contaminated the property of Mr. Jaime Herrera, from which they enter the stream, which flows into the Napo; the pipelines of the Auca field are highly corroded and have exceeded their useful lifespan; the gas flare does not have a pilot light … leading to the emission of gases, which contaminate the air of the inhabitants of the sector; the property of Mr. Carlos Chaquinga contains pools of crude that were buried during previous clean-up operations; oil spills … have polluted the stream that supplies the *Kichwa* community of San Carlos; Anaconda Station: gas flare inoperative. Gases are leaked into the atmosphere without being burned; an oil spill beside the road has not been remediated; two oil spills have contaminated the community of *Voluntad de Dios* (Will of God); a buried pool of crude is leaking into neighboring plots; a pipeline burst beside the home of Mr. Segundo Jobo, setting fire to the house; Armadillo Well: spill at 300 meters … spill at 500 meters … spill at km 7.5 … all affecting the stream [that runs through the *finca*] of *El Encanto* (Enchantment); an oil spill

> led to the burning of the area; the fumes from the gas flare affect the students of the nearby school; the leaking of perforation muds has caused the water to emit strong odors; when the reinjection system fails [the formation waters] are discharged into a lake, affecting streams that flow into the Rumiyacu River; the pipeline … has produced various spills … which have affected a significant extension of the righthand side of the road, the natural gradient of which drains into the streams that are tributaries of the Tiputini River; oil has leaked from the pipeline … into a marsh from which a stream leads to the *Rio Cristal* (Crystal River) … a clean-up operation has yet to be conducted.[18]

The letter accompanying the report concluded that "Owing to the grave contamination suffered by our province, we are being transformed into the living dead (*nos estamos convertiendo en muertos vivientes*)." And at the same time, the oil that was being sucked out of here was feathering the nests of corrupt politicians and boosting the share prices of multinational corporations. By the early 1990s, people were reaching the end of their tether. At around this time, Gonzalo Plazarte was working on his family *finca.* A Black kid from the coast, he had grown up on the Savage Road. He liked to listen to his transistor radio while he worked, but you couldn't get any Ecuadorian stations here. The only thing he could pick up was a Columbian pirate station broadcast by the FARC – the *guerrilla.* Like most inhabitants of the region, he had little formal education and scant knowledge of national politics. But the station was inspiring:

> If you're in your *finca*, far from everything, and you turn on your radio, and you hear the greetings sent by the leaders, the warriors, and so on … . It makes you feel like – "Yes, that is revolution! People fighting for their land! People fighting for their ideals!"[19]

Gonzalo Plazarte was not the only one thinking in these terms. Throughout the Amazon, the worsening conditions and growing sense of injustice were generating increasing opposition to the government and the oil companies. In his words: "We began to demand our rights. We began to demand basic services. Because we saw that it was unjust that the oil all flows out of here, and nothing remains to benefit the people." The sparse population of the region meant that their votes counted for nothing in national elections. And its remoteness meant that the media ignored them too. They were voiceless and invisible. From the perspective of the state, the only thing that mattered about this increasingly apocalyptic place was the oil that flowed out of it. And the oil mattered a lot – it sustained the entire national economy and pumped 400,000 barrels a day into the thirsty veins of the world market. The line of attack was obvious: stop the oil at its source. This, of course, was easier said than done. The oil wells were under armed guard. But the roads were not. Two or three days without supplies getting in to feed the wells – diesel for the generators, lubricant for the pumps, chemicals for the separation tanks, and so on – and the engineers would have no choice but to shut them down. And so, the strategy of the "paralyzation" was born. The blockade. The *paro*. It was simple: barricade a road with trees, earth, rubble, or whatever you can get our hands on, and stop anyone who tries to move it out of the way. Within hours, a long line of oil tankers, worker buses, and supply trucks will have built up. Soon production will start to dip. And suddenly the world will know that you exist.

It worked. Before long, *paros* were springing up across the region. They were swiftly met with military repression. But they would melt away into the jungle only to erupt again. To bring them to an end, the government and the oil companies signed agreements promising to provide the basics of modernity – electricity, water, classrooms, clinics, fertilizers, paved roads, and labor rights. And if they didn't come through on their promises? *Paro!* At first – in the 1990s – the *paros* were small and fragmented. Individual communities fighting for specific things. But they quickly grew in strength and organization. In 1999, the expanding population of the region led to the creation of the new province of Orellana. Two years later, communities throughout Orellana joined forces with those of the neighboring province to create the Bi-Provincial Assembly of Orellana and Sucumbíos (ABP). The two provinces jointly accounted for the vast majority of Ecuadorian oil production, and the ABP was determined to turn this to the advantage of the people. Over the next few years, the movement launched a series of region-wide *paros*, which were increasingly powerful, and which repeatedly forced the government and the oil companies to the negotiating table.[20]

The communities of the *Vía Auca* played a leading role in this Amazonian rebellion. Despite their multiple cultures, races, and ethnicities, and despite the serious tensions and conflicts that continued to exist between them, these communities became increasingly united through the organization and execution of the *paros*. Each was composed of the most marginal and subaltern elements of their own cultures – the landless, the displaced, the excommunicated, the enslaved. Together they formed a community of the dispossessed. They had all been willing to stake everything on the wild bet of moving to this perilous frontier. And they had all managed to survive in this extreme situation. This common attitude and shared experience gave them a collective character of reckless courage and anarchic solidarity. In Plazarte's words:

> We had a revolutionary spirit … We were even ready to take up arms in our struggle … Because this place was turning into a no-man's land. What could we hope for? Prison, death, or the jungle – survival through struggle (*sobrevivir luchando*) … It's one thing to fight tooth and nail (*con patas y manos*) to feed your family … And it's another thing to fight for your ideals. [But] for us, at that time, it was both these things at once. It was our ideal, and it was our necessity. Either fight or die in the trench fighting. That's how it was for us here. We had no alternative.[21]

*****

On August 15, 2005, the ABP launched the biggest *paro* in the history of the Ecuadorian Amazon. Like other roads throughout the region, the *Vía Auca* was blockaded at several crucial choke points. Communities operated shift systems, with one-third of their members performing an eight-hour shift on the barricades every 24 hours. Traders and restaurant owners donated food and water to the frontlines, and communal kitchens and sleeping areas were set up underneath black plastic tarpaulins. Everyone was united. In the words of one militant: "We shut down all the oil wells! … I mean everyone, all the communities everywhere – we shut it all down! … Everyone worked together, and we paralyzed the two provinces of Orellana and Sucumbíos."[22]

A State of Emergency was declared, in which all civil rights were suspended throughout both provinces. The army attacked the barricades with teargas and rubber bullets. But the *paro* held firm. The confrontations were particularly intense on the Savage Road, where militants responded to the repression by burning the vehicles of the oil companies, hijacking oil wells and pumping stations, and forcing the engineers to shut down production. They captured two police informants and took them into the jungle, where they stripped them naked and covered them in honey, and then tied them to a tree and left them overnight. Thousands of ants descended on them to feed upon the honey. They were cut free in the morning and fled into the forest, with the laughter of the renegades ringing in their ears.[23]

By August 18, oil production had been reduced from 400,000 barrels a day to just 10,500, forcing the government to take the unprecedented step of suspending oil exports. Negotiations started three days later, and on August 25, the government and ten oil companies signed a historic agreement with the ABP. It included the direct transfer of 16 percent of corporate income tax from the oil companies to the two provincial administrations, the paving of roads throughout the region, and the elimination of outsourcing (*tercerización*), through which the companies had previously avoided the legal obligation to distribute a percentage of local profits to their employees.[24]

These accords were quickly implemented under threat of further blockades, and cash finally began flowing to the provincial governments of the northern Amazon. Wages increased, the main roads began to be paved, and leading figures in the ABP were given positions in government. As a consequence, the radicalism of the region began to decline. But things were different on the Savage Road. None of these improvements had reached this remote frontier, and the August *paro* had reinforced its rebel spirit and solidified its unity. The presidents of the four parishes along the road – Dayuma, El Dorado, Taracoa, and Inés Arango – were battle-hardened militants, who had organized their jurisdictions under the collective name of the Parishes of South Orellana (PSO). The PSO was led by Jhon Rosero, president of Dayuma, which was the largest and most influential of the four parishes. Rosero was a young Colombian immigrant, who was already a veteran of many *paros*. He had a bullet lodged in his leg from the time he came under fire by the army when trying to seize a pumping station, and he had led his first *paro* when he was just 18. They had confronted the soldiers and stolen their teargas. Then they went to the oil camp, launched the teargas at the offices, and sat back and laughed as the managers ran choking into the street.[25]

Jhon Rosero convinced the PSO to continue the strategy of *paros* that had been abandoned by the ABP. But the nature of their enemy was about to change. One of the candidates for the national presidential election of 2006 was Rafael Correa Delgado, a left-wing economist running for a newly created party called *Alianza PAIS* (Alliance of the Proud and Sovereign Homeland). Unlike previous presidential candidates, who had ignored the Amazon, Correa made repeated visits to the region, in which he promised to implement the ABP Accords "down to the last comma."[26] He was received with great enthusiasm. In the words of one member of the ABP: "When he arrived, it was like receiving a god who had come to rescue the region."[27]

But Rosero was a member of Pachakutik, a more established left-wing party with close connections to the national Indigenous movement, and he viewed Correa's promises with skepticism. Correa went on to win the presidency. But while the rest of the country was celebrating his inauguration in January 2007, the Savage Road welcomed him with a *paro*, in which the PSO repeated their demand for "the immediate paving of the road, in accordance with the agreement signed by the transnational oil companies and the ABP."[28]

The long-awaited paving of the road began soon afterwards. Correa, it seemed, was as good as his word. But meanwhile, tensions were building in the isolated region of El Pindo, two hours' drive down a rough road that branched off the *Vía Auca*. The region lay on the boundary of the Yasuni National Park, in the area thought to be inhabited by the *Tagaeri* and the *Taromenane*. It was the site of two oilfields – Block 14 and Block 17, both of which overlapped with the Intangible Zone, where oil exploration and extraction were supposedly prohibited. But oil knows no rules, and in 2006, the concession for both blocks had been granted to the Chinese company PetroOriental.

El Pindo had been settled in the late 1980s by *Kichwa*, *Shuar*, and mestizo communities, who had fought it out for this last corner of available land, trading shots along the disputed borders of their *fincas*. But the multiple *paros* of the intervening years had transformed them into a unified force. On June 27, 2007, they launched a *paro* against PetroOriental, demanding jobs for unemployed local workers. All 18 communities of El Pindo participated, with the backing of the PSO and the Prefecture of Orellana, which like the parish council of Dayuma was held by Pachakutik and opposed to Correa.

The *paro* posed a serious problem for the Correa regime. The oil price was booming, and Correa was following Hugo Chávez in Venezuela and Evo Morales in Bolivia in using natural resource rents to drive the redistributive development project known as "twenty-first century socialism."[29] On the one hand, he needed to keep the oil flowing to fund the project. But on the other, the project was supposed to defend the Ecuadorian people against the neocolonialism of foreign corporations. Now a group of Ecuadorians was blocking the extraction of oil by a foreign corporation. There was a major contradiction here. A deadlock. But PetroOriental demanded military support, and Correa chose his side and decided to go in hard. On the second day of the *paro*, while the militants were maintaining the blockades, the army attacked the town of Pindo Central where women were preparing food for the barricades. The soldiers broke into the humble homes, kicking down the doors, looting whatever was worth taking and smashing up the rest. Teargas canisters were launched at point blank range into the houses, one of which fractured a woman's skull, while new-born babies and the old and sick remained trapped inside.

This indiscriminate violence was intended to bring the *paro* to a rapid conclusion. Instead, it triggered an insurrection. A group of soldiers accused of launching the attack were captured and doused in gasoline and were lucky to escape with their lives.[30] According to a report submitted by PetroOriental to the public prosecutor of Orellana, another group were ambushed by insurgents who "emerged from the depths of the jungle and began shooting at the soldiers."[31] Two days later, an oil company vehicle was allegedly "impacted by firearm projectiles fired by demonstrators." The army responded by storming the *Shuar* community of Tiguano. Houses were invaded, possessions were destroyed, and teargas and live rounds were deployed. This provoked a further retaliation, in which the PetroOriental report claims that "a group of demonstrators fired shotgun shells, injuring eight members of the Ecuadorian army … who had to be evacuated to the city of Quito."

In the judgment of Jhon Rosero, the situation was "close to civil war."[32] The entire area was under military lockdown. But the *paro* continued until July 3, when the army attacked the central stronghold of Santa Rosa, opening fire with assault rifles and launching over six hundred teargas canisters at the town. They were met with fierce resistance. The rebels defended the barricades with shotguns, dynamite, and Molotov cocktails. In the ensuing shootout, one *colono* took a bullet in the shoulder, paralyzing his arm. Another was shot in the face, the bullet ripping through his molars on its way out the other side. Seven soldiers were also injured in the battle, and a bridge was burned to the ground on the outskirts of the town. By nightfall, most of the community had escaped into the jungle, where they remained in hiding for the next two days. But a handful of rebels held the fort. Guadalupe Llori, radical prefect of Orellana and a key figure in the ABP, crossed the military lines under cover of darkness, arriving in Santa Rosa at 2am, where she found them scared but resolute, armed with machetes, spears, and shotguns.[33]

The next day Llori published an open letter demanding the immediate withdrawal of troops from the region and condemning Correa for his "shameful silence" in the face of the repression.[34] Correa's response came in a televised speech to the nation. It was unrepentant and unambiguous:

> The *comuneros* ambushed our soldiers! They came out of the jungle, fired on them with shotguns, and went back into the jungle. They burned down a bridge – a bridge that belongs to all Ecuadorians! They threw sticks of dynamite, Molotov cocktails. Go and see for yourselves! … They want to seize the oil installations, stop oil production … We cannot accept any more *paros*

> … They have come to an end with this government *compañeros* … Enough! Enough of this anarchy![35]

Correa had squared the circle. His government was defending the Ecuadorian people *and* the foreign corporations against a common enemy: the motley crew of the Savage Road. And this frontier proletariat was up for the fight. They had never really been part of the nation anyway. They had always been the flotsam, the dregs, the cockroaches ground into the dirt. That's why they had ended up on the *Vía Auca* in the first place. Since then, all they had received from the government and the oil companies was pollution, exploitation, and the occasional kicking. And now they had proven that they could give as good as they get. So why not? Bring it on!

*****

Following the conflict in El Pindo, the paving of the *Vía Auca* came to an abrupt halt. It had only just begun after years of broken promises, and now the government suddenly pulled the funding. Under the circumstances, this could only be interpreted as an act of collective punishment and open provocation. On November 1, 2007, Jhon Rosero sent a letter to the chief of police of Orellana. The letter was introduced with "A revolutionary and combative greeting." It set out plans for a massive *paro*, which would include all 82 communities of the region and would once again demand the immediate paving of the road. It concluded with a declaration: "The *pueblos* of [south Orellana] are the force of our region … Today, tomorrow, and forever. Long live the revolution and comandante Che Guevara! *Hasta la victoria siempre!*"[36]

The *paro* began on November 25 in Dayuma, the largest town on the Savage Road. Dayuma was an improvised settlement of a couple thousand inhabitants – mainly mestizo, *Shuar*, and Afro-descendant – about 30 miles from Coca. Wooden shacks with tin roofs and huts built out of concrete block, huddled in steep gorges and perched on awkward hillsides. The road ran right through the middle of the place, alongside a tangled mass of oil pipelines weaving under and around a strip of simple shops and basic bars. The town was founded in 1986 and named after the *Huaorani* woman who first established contact with American missionaries back in 1958. By the time of the *paro*, Dayuma was "one of the poorest places in the country … The odd general store. One or two cantinas for the oil workers … Trucks raising clouds of dust … and a population without water or electricity."[37]

But Dayuma was also the organizational center of the recent uprisings, and a point through which the entire oil industry had to pass on its way to and from the multiple blocks and fields to the south. As such, it was the perfect place to start the *paro*. At 2pm, according to a police report, the bridge at the entrance to Dayuma was barricaded with rubble, stolen oil pipes, and burning tires, in an operation led by Gonzalo Plazarte.[38] At 10:30pm, rebels armed with dynamite seized control of Auca Sur, the main pumping station south of Dayuma. They overpowered the security guards and shut the station down. During the night, further blockades were set up on feeder roads, and masked gangs closed down multiple oil wells.[39] Meanwhile, the police report primly noted that "alcoholic beverages were being consumed by the demonstrators" on the barricade outside Dayuma and observed that "gunshots and explosions could be heard throughout the night, but no-one on the bridge could be identified, as they had their faces covered with shirts and balaclavas."[40]

The carnival continued the next day. An oil company vehicle was overturned and set alight, the water supply for an oil camp was sabotaged, a ditch was dug across a feeder road, and more wells were shut down. Soldiers worked all night to fill the ditch back in, but at dawn the next day a truckload of renegades showed up and dug it out again. That afternoon, a military vehicle was detained on the bridge into Dayuma by masked men "who shouted that they were going to burn the vehicle."

Oil production had once again been shut down across the region. On November 28, Jhon Rosero led a delegation to Quito to open negotiations with the government. Meanwhile the conflict continued to intensify. That afternoon, according to a second police report, "Eighty individuals with their faces covered" attacked a military convoy, firing shotguns and throwing sticks of dynamite, which resulted in the injury of five soldiers.[41] The following evening, a meeting was held in Dayuma's grandly named "coliseum" – a concrete volleyball court covered by a corrugated metal roof. The meeting was led by Gonzalo Plazarte and Wilmer Armas, vice-president of the parish council of Dayuma. Addressing the crowd from Quito via a mobile phone that Armas held against a megaphone, Rosero announced that the negotiations had failed. According to a police informant who was present at the scene, Rosero "incited those present to continue the *paro*, and to realize more radical acts against state property and the armed forces."

That night, Correa imposed a State of Emergency throughout the province of Orellana. At 8:30 the next morning, armored vehicles carrying four hundred heavily armed soldiers arrived at the entrance of Dayuma. They seized Wilmer Armas at the barricade. He was thrown into the back of a truck, where he was beaten and teargassed. As this was happening, there was an explosion under the bridge. It had apparently been boobytrapped with dynamite in preparation for an occasion of this kind. The bridge held firm. But it was filled with soldiers, one of whom was injured in the blast. At the same time, shots rang out, and a cop was hit by buckshot in the thigh. Now things really kicked off. The army invaded the town, firing rubber bullets and live rounds, breaking doors and windows, setting off teargas canisters inside the houses, destroying furniture and possessions, and beating men, women, and children, while helicopters launched clouds of teargas over the rusted rooftops of the town.

By midday, the police could report that Dayuma was "completely calm, under the vigilant custody of the police and the military, in accordance with the State of Emergency legislation."[42] Twenty-five men were detained and imprisoned on charges of sabotage and terrorism. A few days later Guadalupe Llori was arrested on the same charges and would spend the next 11 months in a high-security jail, obliging her to resign as prefect of Orellana. This time there would be no signing of accords between ministers, oil executives, and rebel leaders to mark the conclusion of the *paro*. In a televised address to the nation, Correa justified the crackdown:

> Get rid of that romantic image of Robin Hoods … defending their jungle! … What is happening in the Amazon is being caused by … *colonos* who have arrived from other parts of the country … because they thought "There's money here. Let's extort the oil companies" … Many of them are hitmen. Terrorists. With dynamite, with bullets, they have received our security forces, who have been obliged to respond. There are horrific photographs in the media, as if there was an excessive use of force. There was nothing of the kind. [The security forces] had to defend themselves because they were being attacked. They are terrorists who use dynamite, rifles, cartridges, shotgun shells etcetera. They have installed a reign of terror! Other governments have tolerated it, and they think that my government will tolerate it. Don't fool yourselves! *Señores*, the anarchy is finished! The party is over! Law, order, and the interests of all Ecuadorians will prevail over the shameless few![43]

Correa was right in a way. The motley crew of the Savage Road did not conform to the dominant leftist image of Indigenous Amazonians defending the rights of a sacred Mother Nature. They were a community of the dispossessed, driven from all corners of the country and beyond. And they were not passive victims of circumstance, grateful for any scraps that might fall from the table of the oil companies. They were proletarian renegades, who did not shirk from forcibly asserting their right to benefit from the resources beneath their feet. The repression had been brutal, and their unity had been shattered. But in the words of the rebel leader Jhon Rosero: "The spirit of struggle is sown in the heart and blood of the people of the Savage Road."[44] And if he thought that this spirit had been defeated, then the president of Ecuador was very much mistaken.

3 The Drop That Spilled the Glass

Ten years later. In the town at the entrance to the Savage Road, people spoke of how things used to be. During the boom, they said, Coca had been full of makeshift brothels where Colombian strippers swung from scaffolding poles, and underground casinos where the oil men played for prizes of sexual favors and bottles of single malt whiskey. There was so much cash flying around that they didn't know what to do with it. One guy who got rich built a five-story shopping mall with a bowling alley and a multiscreen cinema and then let it stand empty. Another bought a scrapped airplane, stuck it on a flatbed barge, mounted speakers in the turbines and turned it into a floating nightclub called "Nautical Rumba." That kind of thing.

But then the oil price crashed. The companies stopped drilling. And that meant they stopped hiring and they stopped paying their bills. The brothels and casinos shut down. The strippers slipped back across the border. And the airplane was hauled up on the riverbank and abandoned. Once the cash had gone, the people looked around and realized that nothing had really changed. Despite all his promises, Correa had provided little for this town, or for the province in general. A couple of understaffed schools, a poorly equipped hospital, and a spectacular new bridge over the Napo, which everyone agreed was of greater benefit to the oil companies than to themselves. That was all they had received for the millions of barrels that had flowed out of here. No one knew exactly how much cash all that oil would have amounted to. But Enrique Morales – a central member of the Bi-Provincial Assembly of Orellana and Sucumbíos (ABP), who had led the negotiations that concluded the legendary *paro* of August 2005, and who now worked for the provincial government – estimated it at over $18 billion in 2013 alone.[1]

That had been the high point of the boom, Morales explained – the year before the crash. The oil price had peaked in 2014 at $120 a barrel, and then began to slide, bottoming out at $23 a barrel two years later. Now, without the petrodollars to sustain it, the government was disintegrating into a morass of crisis and corruption. In June 2016, the publication of the Panama Papers had revealed a massive embezzlement scheme at the heart of the state oil company, Petroecuador. The managing director, Carlos Pareja, had fled the country. From exile, he had implicated the vice-president of Ecuador, Jorge Glas, in an even more extensive network of bribery and theft. Correa had so far escaped these allegations. But the

DOI: 10.4324/9781003345879-3

constitution prevented him from running for re-election in 2017. His handpicked successor, Lenín Moreno, had scraped to victory. But following his inauguration in May 2017, Moreno had abandoned twenty-first century socialism and was shamelessly courting transnational capital. He justified this apparent betrayal by launching a campaign against the corruption of the Correa regime. By the time I arrived in the country in August 2017, Correa was in exile, Pareja was in jail, and Glas had been stripped of the vice-presidency and placed under criminal investigation.[2]

Morales paused his summary to let the obscenity sink in. From his office in the center of Coca, we looked out across the sea of rusted tin roofs that stretched toward the river. All in all, he concluded, "The ten years of the Correa presidency have signified a huge step backward for the people of Orellana."[3] This was due not only to the decadence and profligacy of the regime and its failure to use the oil for the development of the region, but also to its destruction of the radical political organization of the province. Following her release from prison, Guadalupe Llori had been welcomed as a returning hero, and was promptly re-elected as prefect of Orellana. But the crackdown in Dayuma had achieved its desired effect. Since then, there had been no further *paros* of any significance, and resistance had been reduced to the occasional minor protest launched by an isolated community here and there. Many of the leaders of the *paros* had been bought off with backhanders and salaried positions. The so-called "community relations officers" of the state and private oil companies had become experts in the dark arts of divide and rule, building clientelist relationships with Indigenous leaders and spreading rumors designed to turn one group against another. And anyone who dared to cause any trouble for the oil companies was immediately accused of sabotage and terrorism, leading to interminable court cases, unaffordable legal bills, and potential jail time.

The next day, I caught an early morning bus heading down the Savage Road. I wanted to talk to the old leaders in Dayuma – to get their angle on the way things had panned out. The bus crossed the bridge over the Napo, the silent immensity of the river shining in the silver light of dawn. We passed the military base on the far side of the bridge, from which the government used to dispatch convoys to crush the *paros*. The chants of marching soldiers drifted up from the parade ground. Beyond them, the somber jungle stretched impassively downriver to the east.

*****

The bus driver cranks up the cumbia, and we turn onto the *Vía Auca*. Thick fog hanging low over half-cleared land. The road was finally paved a few years ago. But it is already falling apart. The single-lane bridges were never replaced, and people still die on them. We drive past stunted coffee plantations, blackened gas flares, and pastures grazed by thin cattle. Past low concrete houses and wooden huts painted with the faded slogans of political parties. Past women washing clothes in a sluggish brown river. Past an endless flow of corroded pipelines entangled in the undergrowth, and the ragged remains of countless propaganda billboards that once announced the development and modernity that lay just around the corner.

But then we enter Block 61. The Auca oilfield. And suddenly everything changes. All along the roadside, the red earth has been churned up for the laying of new pipelines and the construction of new feeder roads. Here and there, in the distance, the head of a huge drilling rig rears above the jungle canopy. Everywhere, they are drilling new wells, building new platforms, and replacing obsolete extraction systems. The rest of the region might be dead, but Block 61 is booming.

Block 61 is one of the "Crown Jewels" of the Ecuadorian oil industry. In 2015, it contained 379 wells, and was pumping around 65,000 barrels a day, or 19 percent of national production.[4] When he first ran for office, Correa had sworn never to sell the Crown Jewels.[5] But by June 2015, the oil crash had brought his government to its knees, and he was struggling to forestall a full-blown fiscal crisis. The 2017 election was fast approaching, and the imposition of austerity would have guaranteed defeat. The only way to cover the massive shortfall in oil revenues without cutting expenditure was to keep taking on more debt. Correa had lost the confidence of the bond markets with a partial default back in 2008. Since then, he had repeatedly turned to China for credit, running up a debt of over $17 billion, much of which was in the form of loans-for-oil contracts.[6] But most of the oil production for the next few years had already been mortgaged in this way, and now Correa needed to regain favor with the bond markets. A $680 million bond repayment would fall due in six months' time.[7] If he were to have any chance of finding buyers for fresh bonds, the payment would have to be made. But the government had no means of doing so. Correa was staring down the barrel of default.

These circumstances forced Correa to break his campaign promise and sell Block 61. He wouldn't sell it exactly. Instead, in a political sleight of hand, he would pursue a public–private partnership that would pay a foreign company a fixed price per barrel for the process of extraction. Block 61 was a mature field. There were only 300 million barrels of oil left of the original 4 billion, and they were increasingly difficult to access. Production levels were starting to dip, at a moment when the government was desperate for extraction to expand. The field was operated by the state oil company, Petroamazonas, which was on the verge of bankruptcy and incapable of making the necessary investments.[8] The partner company would take over the extraction process, investing in the technology and infrastructure required to drive up production, and sealing the deal with an immediate $1 billion loan that would allow the government to make the bond repayment and avoid default.[9]

On December 14, 2015, one day before the bond repayment fell due, Petroamazonas signed a 20-year contract for Block 61 with Schlumberger, the largest oilfield services company in the world. Schlumberger agreed to invest $4.9 billion over the duration of the contract, including the initial $1 billion loan. It would increase the production of Block 61 from 65,000 to 85,000 barrels a day, through technological upgrading and the drilling of 172 new wells. Most of this work would be undertaken in the first three years of the project, involving an investment of $1.1 billion during this period alone. Work would begin in January 2016.[10]

The $1 billion loan came through and the bond repayment was made.[11] The managing director of Petroamazonas celebrated the moment with a triumphant speech, which sought to present this major step in the privatization of the Ecuadorian oil industry as a proud embodiment of twenty-first century socialism:

> We welcome the multinational Schlumberger to Block 61 as a contractor of world renown, which will help us transform our potentialities into roads, hospitals, schools, quality services, and other public works that will provide dignity to Ecuadorian lives. We have overcome the old discourse of those who criticize alliances with the private sector. Make no mistake about it! A public-private alliance is a tool that in good, transparent hands, will bring great improvements to the nation.[12]

In fact, the deal had been negotiated in secret by Carlos Pareja and was signed behind closed doors by Jorge Glas – the ringleaders of corruption in the Correa administration. And the terms themselves were criminal. In 2012, Correa had cut a similar deal with Schlumberger for the operation of the nearby Shushufindi field – another of the Crown Jewels, and the only field more productive than Block 61 itself. That was at the height of the oil boom, and he had been able to set the terms. But this time Schlumberger held all the cards and had driven a hard bargain. The company would be paid an average tariff of $26 a barrel, at a time when Ecuadorian crude was selling for $27 a barrel. According to Petroamazonas, the cost of production in Block 61 was no more than $10 per barrel, including capital investments. And $7 of the tariff charged for each barrel was slated as repayment for the $1 billion loan. But that still only accounted for $17 of the $26-a-barrel price tag. In other words, Schlumberger was making at least $9 of clear profit on every barrel extracted, while under actual prices, Ecuador stood to make just $1 per barrel.[13]

Furthermore, in marked contrast to other similar contracts (such as the one for the Shushufindi field), Schlumberger was not only being paid for the barrels corresponding to the expanded production resulting from its investments. It was being paid for every single barrel produced, allowing it to profit from prior investments made by the state oil company.[14] According to one estimate, Schlumberger stood to make a profit of $6.4 billion over the duration of the contract.[15] In the words of the investigative journalist who first revealed the terms of the contract, the deal amounted to a "lottery for Schlumberger, crumbs for Ecuador."[16] An ex-energy minister agreed, publicly describing it as "an early Christmas for the company and a national disgrace."[17]

This was the story behind the construction work that could be seen from the bus window on the road to Dayuma. Not for the first time, a multinational corporation had used its financial power to convince a weak and corrupt government to allow it to plunder the natural resources of an obscure extractive frontier But something was amiss. The place was clearly in the throes of a massive transformation.

The roadsides were filled with building materials and digging machinery. But the piles of pipelines and stacks of cement were undisturbed, and the machines stood empty. Where were all the workers?

*****

Rounding a sharp corner, the road suddenly dips to cross a stream. I catch a glimpse of a group of men under the bridge. An albino man is holding one end of a long metal chain. "They're waiting for someone," the guy sitting beside me says. The bus grinds down through the gears and growls up a steep slope onto an open hilltop. To the left, a solitary gas flare roars in the middle of the jungle. To the right, a huge oil camp has been carved into the red earth. This is the *Obrador Central* – the operational center of the company subcontracted by Schlumberger to rebuild Block 61. Its offices are housed here, along with trucks, excavators, materials, and enough buses to transport 1,100 workers to and from their homes and the construction sites. Behind the *Obrador*, the town of Dayuma clings stubbornly to the hillside.

We descend the hill toward the town. Past the luridly painted facade of Pink Booty (*Botín de Rosa*) – a brothel built to capture oil workers with their monthly salaries before they can make it home from work. At the bottom of the hill, we reach the bridge into Dayuma – the one the rebels allegedly boobytrapped with dynamite back in 2007. The bridge has been closed for maintenance, and a diversion leads us onto a dirt track that runs around to the right past the company gates. They are shut and surrounded by high metal walls, topped with razor wire and security cameras. A small group of workers is gathered outside. "It looks like a strike," the man beside me says. On the way into town, I see another group of people talking with two men in military uniform. Something is definitely going on.

The bus drops me at the top of the hill, in the center of town. It is just past 8am. I was told to get here early if I wanted to find a room. Dayuma is a boomtown now, and places fill up fast. The first two hotels I try are full, so I search a little further from the center. One block off the main drag and I'm already on the edge of town. I take the last room in the Hotel Guerrero, which stands beside an exhausted oil platform. A brand-new place with a veneer of petro-decadence: fake marble floors, mirrored windows, and yellow stains already running through cracked concrete walls. It's just been fumigated, and the floor is strewn with cockroaches – some dead and some still twitching.

The rest of Dayuma is still an improvised and impoverished place, perched on ridges and buried in gorges. Trucks carrying pipelines and machinery heave their way along the narrow high-street in a constant cloud of dust. I gulp down a couple cups of instant coffee in a hut on the roadside, then cross the road to the headquarters of the parish council. Green slime oozes from the rotten concrete walls. I enter the building behind a tall man in an expensive shirt. We sit on the same bench, and silently wait our turn to speak to the president of the parish council, Judith Hidalgo. The place is filled with parishioners – mestizo, *Shuar*, *Kichwa*. Judith makes a point of leaving the two of us until last. She was elected president in 2014. Like Jhon Rosero, the rebel leader who was president during the era of the *paros*, she represents Pachakutik. As a matter of fact, she's married to the guy. He works here as well, and the general *machista* consensus is that he's still running the show.

At last, the waiting room is empty except for me and the expensively attired man. Judith Hidalgo emerges from her office and waves us both inside. She is fashionably dressed in an orange jumpsuit, looking more like a metropolitan socialite than what the same *machista* consensus would lead one to expect of the president of a renegade parish on a rugged oil frontier. But Judith is a seasoned militant, who played a leading role in the campaign for the release of the prisoners following the military crackdown in 2007. A huge Ecuadorian flag stands behind her, alongside a stash of *Huaorani* spears. The man who entered with me introduces himself as the head of security for Schlumberger. There is a strike underway, and he wants to know what's going on. Without looking at me, Judith begins to respond. She must assume that I'm with him. And he must think that I am known to her. Before I can say anything, she is already telling him that the strike began a few days ago. It has been organized by the works council of the construction company. But there are only a few workers involved. It's nothing for him to worry about, she says, although he should bear in mind that the oil companies have bled this place dry for decades and have never given the people anything in return. He smiles and nods in amiable agreement. Then Judith turns to me for my reaction. I point out that I did not come here with him. She throws her hands in the air in confusion. The man from Schlumberger doesn't stop smiling. He thanks her and leaves.

Now Judith wants to know who the hell I am. Luckily, I have a card up my sleeve. I've just published a book here in Ecuador – a critique of the Correa regime.[18] It ends with a quote from her husband, and I have a copy for him. A moment later Jhon Rosero marches in – a middle-aged mestizo, with a brooding self-assurance that looks like it could easily slide into belligerence. He is suspicious of me at first, and seems to have forgotten that I interviewed him a year or so before. But he brightens up a little when he sees his words in print, and gruffly motions me into his adjacent office. The room is dark and bare, with a solitary desk filled with a clumsy old computer. He stabs his forefingers into the keyboard for a couple of minutes. Then he sits back and gives me the lowdown on the strike.

*****

The trouble began with the contract for Block 61. Ecuador undoubtedly got ripped off. But the same oil crisis that had forced the country to the brink of default was also killing Schlumberger. In the fourth quarter of 2015, while the contract was being negotiated, Schlumberger's revenue had fallen by 39 percent. Major projects were being canceled around the world, and by the time the contract was signed in December 2015, the company had dismissed 34,000 employees in a single year.[19] The extortionate terms that Schlumberger had forced on Ecuador had been driven less by corporate greed than by a desperate need to squeeze every last dollar out of Block 61 in order to survive. But in its fixation on this objective, Schlumberger had lost sight of a simple fact: Ecuador had no means of paying the company for the oil extracted from the Auca field.[20] Payment was supposed to begin on the day the contract was signed. But by the end of 2016, over one year later, not one single barrel had been paid for, and Ecuador owed Schlumberger over $1 billion in oil revenues, over and above the original $1 billion loan. And to paraphrase a well-known saying about banks, if you owe an oil company that much money then it's the company that has the problem. The tables had been turned, and now it was the company's turn to go, cap in hand, to plead with the Ecuadorian government. In March 2017, the CEO of Schlumberger, Paal Kibsgaard, wrote a letter to Correa, in which he begged the Ecuadorian president for his "personal help" in unblocking the payments. The extent of the debt, he anxiously explained, had forced Schlumberger to "raise additional external borrowings" to finance its operations in Block 61, and was pushing the company to the brink of financial ruin.[21]

Correa remained impervious to his supplications. Behind a vast mahogany desk on the top floor of a gleaming Houston skyscraper, the CEO of Schlumberger seethed with impotent fury. Someone was going to have to pay for this. And as usual, it was going to be the workers. Initially, Schlumberger had subcontracted the construction work for Block 61 to Oil Construction and Services (CPP), which had operated the Shushufindi field on its behalf since 2012. Under Ecuadorian law, this arrangement obliged Schlumberger to pay 3 percent of its profits from the field to the employees of CPP. These payments were called *utilidades*, and were made in April of each year. When CPP began operating in Block 61, it had hired workers on very low wages. But this was accompanied by a verbal promise of big *utilidades* to come in April 2017. CPP was known to pay well in this regard. Workers in the neighboring field of Shushufindi had received pay-outs of as much as $25,000 back in the years of the boom. The workers in Block 61 could look forward to a similar jackpot.

But in June 2016, the operation of Block 61 was quietly taken over by Global Andean Construction (CGA), a company created for this purpose. CPP and CGA were both subsidiaries of Techint – an Italo-Argentine conglomerate comprising six divisions. But whereas CPP was located in the division specializing in oil extraction, CGA was established in the division specializing in public works.[22] This shift in the legal status of the subcontractor from an oil company to a construction company allowed Schlumberger's accountants to save an estimated $31 million on their balance sheets, by silently assuming that the corporation was no longer liable for the payment of *utilidades* in Block 61, despite the fact that its subcontractor had not changed in anything but name.[23]

Of course, none of this was mentioned to the workers. Meanwhile, costs were cut to the bone, and working conditions deteriorated. Low wages, long hours, poor meals, and humiliating treatment by their Argentinian bosses. The workers bit their tongues and kept telling themselves that the *utilidades* would make it all worthwhile. But when April 2017 arrived, their pay slips recorded the same miserable salary as ever. This was one month after Correa had ignored the urgent request for assistance from the CEO of Schlumberger, and it coincided with the company reporting a further 7 percent decline in revenues, which it attributed to Ecuador's continued failure to pay its debts.[24] Schlumberger may have been screwed over by the Ecuadorian government. But at least it had managed to claw back a bit of cash by ripping off the workers of the Savage Road.

The failure to pay *utilidades* was a flagrant betrayal of trust. But more importantly, it was supposed to be illegal. One of the great victories of the ABP uprising back in August 2005 had been the abolition of *tercerización* – a subcontracting practice through which oil companies had avoided paying *utilidades* to their workers. This abolition had been enshrined in law in 2008. From the perspective of the workers, the shift from CPP to CGA constituted a clear example of *tercerización*, and a blatant violation of this law. They immediately launched a wildcat strike in protest, which lasted for four days. On the fifth day, the strike leaders were fired and charged with sabotage and terrorism – the accusation with which the Correa regime systematically stifled dissent.

The repression of the strike leaders was combined with a promise of negotiations with the other workers. Everyone returned to work. But the negotiations never happened, and the conditions remained unchanged. At this point, a group of workers decided to create a *comité de empresa* – a works council, which would have the legal right to strike. The *comité* received legal recognition in June 2017, and within two months, 700 of the 1,100 employees of CGA had joined. On August 22, a small sit-down strike began at the construction site of an oil platform south of Dayuma, demanding the payment of the *utilidades*. The strike was joined by the *Shuar* community of Kapáku, where the platform was located, who had not been adequately compensated by the company, and who now blockaded the bridge at the entrance to their land. Four days later, a group of unemployed laborers from Dayuma also joined the protests. Oil workers, Indigenous communities, and the unemployed … Slowly but surely, almost ten years after the crushing of the *paro* in Dayuma, the motley crew of the Savage Road was taking shape again.

On August 28, the workers not involved in the strike arrived at the camp at 6:30am as usual – most of them feared losing their jobs if they joined the protest, despite many being members of the *comité*. They signed in and boarded the buses that would take them to the building sites. But on the way out of town they found their path blocked by chains stretched across the road. The southern roadblock was manned by the *comuna* of Kapáku, and the northern one by members of the *comité*. That was this morning, and those were the people I had seen hiding under the bridge on my arrival in Dayuma. On their return to the camp the workers had been locked inside. The managers claimed they were concerned for the workers' safety. But in truth they were terrified that the workers would leave and join the strike that was now taking place outside the gates. One thousand workers had been imprisoned by their own management, and all operations had been suspended, just as I had wandered into town.[25]

*****

I have exhausted the scarce reserves of Jhon Rosero's patience, to which I had gained brief access with the gift of my book. He shrugs wearily in response to my next question. He has told me what he knows. If I want more information, I should speak to those involved. He makes a couple calls to let them know I'm on my way. Then he turns back to his computer and resumes his gloomy stabbing of the keys.

It is high noon. The sun has burned off the early morning fog, and the heat is intense. I descend the hill toward the *Obrador Central*. The gates are closed, and the entrance is deserted. The striking workers have sought out the last remaining scraps of shade in a side street between the town and the high wall of the oil camp. But as soon as they catch sight of me, the screeching of the cicadas is drowned out by a barrage of angry voices. They get to their feet and stride down the street toward me. About 40 or 50 of them, I would say. All dressed in the company uniform of blue jeans and denim shirt. They assume that I'm a journalist. And if so, then I'm the first one to have shown his face around here since the start of this situation back in April. They want their story to be told. I explain that I'm not a journalist but an academic researching the region, which they say is good enough for them. I grab my notebook and turn on my recorder. The first worker steps from the crowd to give his testimony. He's in his mid-thirties or so, and is a spokesperson of the *comité*. A mestizo *colono* from the highlands who has lived here almost all his life, he is short and well built, with calloused hands and sun-blasted skin, and a mood that shifts incessantly between exuberance, hilarity, and indignation:

> My name is Luis Barberan. But here we are all the same. Here there are no leaders, there is no president of anything, there are no bosses. We are community. We are *pueblo*. Everyone is here for a single reason. Because the company CGA or Techint – the only reason they have come here is first to cheat us, second to exploit us, third to mistreat us, to insult us. To tell us we are idiots and our mothers are whores. You understand me, right? So, everyone here is sick of all this … They pay us a miserable salary. They only feed us once a day. We [are supposed to] work from 7 in the morning to 4 in the afternoon. That's a lie because we have to leave home at 4:30 in the morning to be here at 6:30 – those of us who live far away … And we don't lay off until 6pm and then sometimes the bosses say "No, you have to finish this [first]. And if you don't stay, I'll report you. And if you don't stay, I'll fire you."[26]

Barberan turns to the group of workers gathered around us: "Isn't that so, my friends? (*No es así compañeros?*)" They roar in agreement. And on top of all that, he says, the company didn't come through with the *utilidades* they had been promised. And now the managers have shut the rest of the workers inside the camp and chained the gates. He turns to his fellow workers again. "What we want, very simply, is for CGA to get out. *Si o no compañeros?*" They respond in boisterous unison: "They must get out!" "And where should they get out of?" Barberan shouts at the top of his voice. "Out of Block 61!" they bellow in reply. He turns back to me and lowers his voice to a growl, speaking slowly and deliberately through gritted teeth:

> The only thing we want is for CGA to leave. We are tired of this. Imagine if I came to your country, to your *pueblo*. And I fucked you over once. And then I fucked you over two, three, four, five, ten times. What are you going to want? Are you going to want me to keep fucking you over? Or are you going to want me to leave?

He steps back, and other workers take turns to give their points of view. Meanwhile, the street fills with people wanting to hear what is being said. A police car pulls up at the end of the road. Two cops get out and silently begin to photograph the scene. The next worker to speak is Jimmy Chamba, another representative of the *comité*. I recognize him as the albino I had seen holding the chain under the bridge. Everyone calls him *Tilapia* – a pale pink fish that is common in these parts. He accuses the bosses of racism. Not toward him, but toward the Indigenous workers. They are subjected to constant insults – "shit for brains, imbeciles, monkeys," and systematically fired after three months – the probation period within which a worker can be dismissed without receiving severance pay.

An Indigenous worker then steps forward. His name is Edison Kapáku, a *Shuar* and a member of the Kapáku clan who have blockaded the bridge at the building site where the sit-down strike began. He seems to be a bit of a dreamer, with an ill-fitting uniform and an absent-minded manner. He is soft-spoken at first and struggles to find the right words. But then he gets into gear, and his voice rises above the crowd:

> Here we are representing … No, we're not representing. Rather, we are here. We are present! Because the company CGA has ground us into the dirt … We don't want foreign companies coming here to give us orders … They come here to fill their pockets, and we pay the cost. Coming to Ecuador is like winning the lottery for them. That's why Ecuador remains in poverty, and especially Dayuma. The oil flows out of Dayuma, and the foreign companies take the money and run.

Now everyone starts talking at once. I scribble down as much as I can. The salary paid to unskilled workers is just $386 a month. And this is a remote oil region where the cost of everything is inflated. It's impossible to raise a family here on less than $700 a month. They work long hours to try to make it up, but are often not paid overtime. In other oil blocks, the work schedule is 14 days on, 14 days off. But here it's 22 days on and 8 days off. Other oil companies provide breakfast and lunch to their workers. But here they only get lunch. It is always meager and often inedible, made from spoiled goods that the company buys at discount prices. The soup is "white water with a piece of potato." The main course is "hard rice and old meat." One worker found maggots crawling in his food. Another describes eating fish which looked OK under its sauce, but which turned out to be rotten. Anyone who complains about any of this is threatened with dismissal and told that there are a hundred people waiting to take their job. And if you say another word, "they pick you up and throw you out, like a dog."

But since the creation of the *comité*, the situation has changed. CGA can't just fire them anymore. And now the management is starting to panic. Barberan swaggers back into the middle of the circle at this point and takes over the story. Techint have sent a representative called Pellegrini from their headquarters in Argentina – "one of the guys who sort out problems for them around the world." Pellegrini emerged from the camp to speak with them not long before I arrived. He began by addressing each of the *comité* representatives by name, praising their individual qualities and emphasizing their value to the company. He then implored them to abandon the strike, for the good of everyone. Finally, he gently explained why it was impossible for CGA to pay *utilidades*. Barberan impersonates Pellegrini in a high-pitched, wheedling voice, to the great amusement of the rest:

> So, the dude starts saying "Look here fellows, you see the problem is the national economy, the deficit, the dollar, the price of oil. We are investing an awful lot of money here, and we have basically come to help you out." "Whatever," I told him, "Very pretty words, Mr. Engineer. Really beautiful. I only have one question: Would you give me one thousand dollars?" He laughs: "Why do you ask?" "Just out of interest. I'll tell you. You wouldn't give me a single cent, let alone one thousand dollars! You expect us to believe that you've come here to invest a shitload of money without any benefit to yourselves? Excuse me, Mr. Engineer, I don't mean to be rude or abusive. In fact, I will thank you. I will even kiss your ass if that's what you want! But only when you have done something good for the workers, for us, for my companions and myself. In the meantime, Mr. Engineer, with the greatest respect, we are going to continue exactly as we are. You have your nice office in Argentina. You travel around spending what we have worked [to produce]. That's what you do. And you make ten times more than we do. And why do they pay you so well? To come here and make us dizzy with your bullshit!"

Pellegrini was speechless. He turned on his highly polished heel and walked stiffly back into the oil camp. That was a couple of hours ago, and there has been no sign of him since. End of story. The workers slap Barberan on the back and wipe away their tears of laughter. But then his phone rings, and the mood shifts. Apparently, the management is trying to move vehicles out of a second gate on the far side of the camp. They have to be stopped. Barberan will head over there with a few others, but they will need support. "Send me people! Send me people!" he shouts into the phone. He revs his motorbike and tells me to jump on behind him. We accelerate past the company gates and tear up the hill, past the brothel and the gas flare and out onto the open hilltop, where a dirt track leads down to the back of the camp. From here, we have a clear view across the installations. We can see dozens of vehicles lined up and motionless. Hundreds of workers in their blue uniforms are gathered behind the main gates. But there is no sign of any vehicle trying to leave from the gate on this side.

Strange … Then things happen very fast. A convoy of police cars and SUVs with tinted windows and no plates comes roaring up the hill and screeches to a halt. A tall man in plain clothes and dark glasses walks quickly toward us, followed by five or six cops. The man points to Barberan and the cops grab him and push him into one of the cars. The convoy drives off at speed. I'm left standing in a cloud of dust, along with a few more workers who have just arrived. One of them gets a call. Jimmy Chamba – *Tilapia* – has just been detained and driven away in the same convoy.

We turn and walk back to the top of the dirt track leading down to the back of the installations. The news spreads fast. The roar of a thousand voices drifts over the jungle like distant thunder. Looking across the camp toward the main entrance, we can see the workers breaking the gates open and surging out onto the Savage Road. We stand there in silence for a moment. Then one of the workers beside me lets out a low whistle. "*Chuta,*" he says, "*Eso fue la gota que derramó el vaso.*" Which roughly translates as: "Holy shit... That was the drop that spilled the glass."

4 Wild Style

We jump back on the motorbikes and hurtle down the hill. The road outside the company gates is filled with oil workers, and their rage is infused with insurrectional delight. It turns out that the stakes of the conflict have been raised even further in the few minutes it has taken us to get here. As the workers were streaming out of the gates, a handful of members of the *Shuar* community of Kapáku rushed past them in the opposite direction. If the company was going to get the cops to take their leaders prisoner, then it was surely only reasonable that they should respond in kind. Not with the help of the cops, of course, but with their own bare hands. They were looking for the detested head of human resources, who they held primarily responsible for the systematic humiliation of the workers in general and the racist denigration of the Indigenous workers in particular. But in the chaos of the moment, he was nowhere to be found. They knew they had to act fast, and so they seized the first manager they saw. This just happened to be the *gerente de operaciones*, Esteban García – the operations manager of CGA and thus the biggest boss of all those stationed at the *Obrador Central*.

García was standing outside his air-conditioned office at the time, where he had been laughing with a couple of sycophantic underlings about the detention of Tilapia and Barberan. The next thing he knew, he was being marched out of the company gates by a gang of furious *indígenas*. A photograph taken on a *Shuar* smartphone shows a tall white man with designer stubble and neatly groomed gray hair. He is looking over his shoulder with an expression of undisguised desperation and is pleading with two stocky *Shuar* men, whose fists are driven firmly into his back. Other *Shuar* men and women are surrounding them and running toward a silver pickup waiting on the road. One of the women is wearing a red T-shirt emblazoned with two blue words in English: "Wild Style."

The truck belongs to the state oil company, Petroamazonas. The *Shuar* flagged it down. Then they hijacked it, threw García in the back, and headed south down the Savage Road, into the depths of the jungle.[1] This isn't just a strike anymore. This is an uprising. And the workers haven't just laid down their tools. They've kidnapped the boss of the company and taken him to an unknown destination to meet an uncertain fate. Everyone is laughing about the sheer audacity of the *Shuar* and enjoying the sweet taste of revenge. But soon we receive news that armored vehicles have been dispatched from the military base in Coca and are approaching

DOI: 10.4324/9781003345879-4

at speed. The soldiers should be here in less than half an hour. This will be the first time since 2007 that the army has entered Dayuma, and everyone knows all about the brutality of that crackdown.

The scene is tense, to say the least. But the line has been crossed, and the workers are determined to hold firm. "We have to strike hard," says one "We'll shut it all down," says another. Then a third worker calls everyone together: "This is a matter for all of us!" he shouts. "We have gotten involved, and now we must continue! If we don't do this now, when will we ever achieve anything?" Cries go up of "Yes!" and "He's right!" "We will stay here!" he continues, "Two truckloads of soldiers are on their way. We need to remain united in this situation, otherwise they will take us one by one."

The decision is unanimous: the workers will hold the line against the army. They will remain here overnight. No one will work the next day, and anyone who attempts to work will be prevented from doing so. Many of those who burst out of the gates a few minutes ago are not members of the *comité* and were not intending to participate in the strike. But the detention of Barberan and Tilapia was a step too far. Now everyone is furious with the company, the government, and especially the cops. One of the workers tells me that "The police always defend the company against the people." Another denounces the fact that "The foreign companies buy the police." And a third insists that "The police are supposed to protect the citizenry, not to attack us in this manner. But you saw how they just took [Barberan] with the point of a finger and threw him [into the car] like a dog."

Everyone is convinced that the police were acting on the instruction of CGA. Several workers saw the cops talking with CGA's security chief immediately before the arrests, and the guy in plain clothes and dark glasses who had led the arrest of Barberan looked more like private security than a cop. This suggests that the head of security for Schlumberger, who had been with me in the office of Judith Hidalgo, must have had a hand in the affair. After all, Barberan and Tilapia were the two leaders I had interviewed, and they had been detained almost immediately after I had spoken to them. In other words, my unwitting arrival on the scene would seem to have been the random spark that had set the whole thing off.

Our speculations are cut short by the arrival of the army, followed by a line of police cars. They stop at the top of the hill, from which point a few dozen soldiers descend on foot, before silently forming a cordon at the curve of the road above the company gates. They wear helmets and bulletproof vests over their camouflage fatigues. They carry riot shields, night sticks, revolvers, and teargas guns and canisters. The workers blocking the road beneath them are unarmed. Some hold hastily scrawled placards: "CGA out of Block 61"; "Workers united in demanding our rights"; and "Our region deserves respect: *Kichwa*, *Shuar*, *Huacrani*," which is held not by *indígenas* but by mestizo *colonos*.

A hush falls over the scene. Fear is etched into the faces of some of the younger workers. But most return the steady gaze of the soldiers. Then, Colonel Wilson Tualombo arrives – the Commander of the Nineteenth Division of the Napo Jungle Brigade. He is in the passenger seat of an unmarked vehicle, which tries to force its way through the crowd. The workers close ranks to block its path. At a signal from the colonel, the soldiers would descend upon them. But instead, the vehicle slowly reverses, and the soldiers gradually retreat to the top of the hill. The tension eases, and the silence is broken by a long-abandoned battle cry: "*Viva el paro!*"

*****

This small initial victory gives confidence to the workers. They begin to allow civilian vehicles to pass, after searching them for hidden cops and soldiers. Several trucks are requisitioned for the cause and sent down the Savage Road to bring reinforcements to the *paro*. There are chants of "*Libertad! Libertad!*" and "We all have rights!" Passengers shout support from the windows of passing buses, amid cries from the workers to "Unite yourself with the people!" Meanwhile, conversation turns to memories of the golden age of the *paros*, although many of these workers were only children at the time. The "terrorist" label with which Correa had demonized the local population back in 2007 has become a badge of honor, and the *paro* in El Pindo is recalled with particular pride. Pedro, a mestizo with a face like a bulldog and hair shaved into a mohawk, says that El Pindo "almost turned into a civil war between soldiers and civilians." Tigrillo – a skinny guy with a missing tooth, who is nicknamed after an Amazonian wildcat – yells "Dayuma is terrorist!" Recalling the battle of El Pindo with relish, Tigrillo describes the injuries inflicted on some of the soldiers: "Those dudes left without their legs! (*Salieron sin piernas esos manes!*)"

These nostalgic reminiscences are interrupted by some bad news: Esteban García, the operations manager of CGA, has been rescued by the police further down the Savage Road. Cops patrolling the southern oilfields blocked the hijacked pickup just a mile or so before the turnoff to the *comuna* of Kapáku. If the *Shuar* had gotten him into their territory, they could have hidden him in the jungle where he never would have been found. But as it was, they accepted defeat and gave up their hostage without a fight. Now the workers have lost their strongest bargaining chip in the campaign for the release of their leaders, and talk immediately turns to storming the oil camp again and seizing another member of the management, several of whom remain trapped inside.

Before they can take any further action in this regard, however, the chief superintendent of the Orellana Police arrives, accompanied by a representative of the Governorship of Orellana – the institution charged with doing the dirty work of the national government at the local level. Pedro, Tigrillo, and other leading figures of the *paro* begin to remonstrate with them, while other workers gather around, filming on their phones, and trying to catch a word or two of what is being said. The Superintendent is a haughty woman in her late fifties or so. For some reason she is out of uniform, and is wearing an immaculate white dress. Her heavy make-up is starting to crack and run in the heat, and she keeps losing her balance in her white stilettos, which are perched precariously on the rounded river stones that surface the road. Her lips are pursed in discomfort, and the debate is handled by the representative of the Governorship – an eager bureaucrat in his early thirties, who sports chunky hipster glasses and is already running to fat. Delivering his message in a pedantic nasal whine, he insists that the company's operations are entirely legal and that the workers' actions in blocking the road are most certainly not.

Pedro shakes his mohawked head in disgust. Turning away from the bureaucrat, he shouts to the workers gathered behind him: "Don't waste your time with it! They're not going to solve anything!" Then another shout comes from up the hill, and several workers turn and start running in that direction, toward a line of police cars that have just pulled up alongside a shuttered restaurant, behind which runs the high fence of the *Obrador Central*. By the time we arrive, the cops have formed a cordon around the cars and the restaurant, from behind which a line of company managers emerges through a hole in the fence. They must have been hiding there, waiting for the distraction caused by the superintendent and the bureaucrat. And now they are making their escape.

Too late! The workers surround the cordon, bellowing a barrage of insults at the furtive managers, who scuttle into the waiting cars. Some of them are visibly trembling with fear. Tigrillo points at them and doubles up with laughter: "Look at them running out like rats!" he shouts in livid jubilation. One worker tries to block the first car but is bundled out of the way by the cops, and the convoy roars away uphill. Just as they had detained the workers, so the police have saved the managers, who are driven at top speed to a luxury hotel in Coca. According to a member of staff at the hotel, the managers refused to stay there, and departed immediately for Quito, babbling about an ambush of the oil camp by spear-wielding cannibals.[2]

*****

Foiled in their attempt to acquire another hostage, the workers return to the company gates and resume their discussion with the pedantic bureaucrat. But no one is in the mood for his nonsense. A few more nasal utterances of incomprehensible legalese, and Olger Naichap has had as much as he can take. Olger is a militant young *Shuar* from the nearby *comuna* of Charapa. He works for CGA on one of the chainsaw gangs, clearing jungle for the oil platforms being constructed throughout Block 61. When he speaks, he spits his words out as if they were on fire. "You say the company is complying with the law – is that not so, my dear sir? (*No es así, mi jefe?*)," he begins, addressing the bureaucrat in a tone of sardonic deference. "What are they complying with, exactly? Are they complying with this?" He kneels down and seizes a worthless rock from the ground as if to indicate the absurdly minimal standards to which CGA is supposedly complying. "Is this just?" he shouts, brandishing the rock above his head. "Or is it unjust?" He straightens up and brings his face close to the bureaucrat, who retreats toward the line of cops behind him. "Slavery is finished!" Olger roars, "I am a *Shuar*!" Within a few words, he has shifted from obsequious politeness to incandescent rage: "Stop enslaving us! We are also Ecuadorians! Don't come here and lie to us!"

His voice is drowned out by shouts of support from the workers, and from one of the *Shuar* women involved in the kidnap of Esteban García, who has just returned from the scene of his release. Linda Kapáku is a middle-aged woman with graying hair, dressed in black leggings, plastic sandals, and a dark blue blouse decorated with white butterflies. Now she takes her turn to berate the bureaucrat: "We are also humans! We also have rights! But we just keep getting poorer!" She points to the cops behind him: "They took two of our leaders as if they were delinquents! Look at them! They come here armed! They may be men, but they are cowards!" She is drowned out in turn by a huge chant of "*Libertad! Libertad! Libertad!*" The bureaucrat emits a little sigh, before resuming in the same tone as before, enunciating each syllable as if addressing a group of children: "This is not our concern. We are here to address the matter of the paralyzation. We are not here to address any labor issues you may have … My role is to explain the illegality [of your actions], nothing more."

The crowd erupts in cacophonous fury at this refusal of the government to consider the causes of the conflict or the question of workers' rights. Clearly, the state is only interested in defending the company and ending the *paro* as quickly as possible. At this point Olger Naichap returns to the center of the stage. Turning to address the crowd, he begins by mimicking the patronizing politeness of the bureaucrat: "This gentleman has come to explain the situation. And it is not as if we are incapable of understanding. So now, what are we going to do?" The response from the crowd is deafening, and the consensus could not be clearer. Olger lets the noise die down, then approaches the bureaucrat, bowing and scraping before him in mock submission: "We have heard you. We have understood you. And with the greatest respect …" He pauses for dramatic effect and turns back triumphantly to the crowd: "We are going to continue our struggle *compañeros! Viva el paro!*"

The crowd roars "*Viva!*" in response. The pedantic bureaucrat blinks and adjusts his tie: "You are not approaching the matter in the correct manner," he sniffs reproachfully. "And every [illegal] action has a [legally] determined sanction. There is nothing that remains for me to say on the matter." But everyone has already stopped listening. He begins to waddle back up the hill. At this moment, an old white man arrives, bandy-legged and mustachioed like a midwestern cowboy, wearing scruffy jeans and T-shirt and a grubby baseball cap. There is great commotion in the crowd, and excited shouts of "*El padre! El padre!*" This is Pablo Gallegos, the legendary Carmelite priest – liberation theologian and veteran mediator of countless *paros* across the Ecuadorian Amazon since the early 1970s. He was a three-hour drive away when he heard about the detentions of Barberan and Tilapia. He jumped on a bus and came straight here. Now he is hobbling grumpily up the hill after the bureaucrat, who sees him coming and starts to shuffle away as fast as his portly form and the steep slope will allow. Gallegos is precisely the person that the bureaucrat didn't want to run into here. He is a fearsome character. An irascible old Basque nationalist with no patience for bullshit of any kind. And unlike the workers, Gallegos knows the law inside out. Before long he has collared the bureaucrat and has him on the ropes.

"Who gave the order?" Gallegos demands, referring to the detention of Tilapia and Barberan. "They were caught red handed (*en delito flagrante*)," the bureaucrat replies. His voice, so self-assured a moment ago, is high-pitched and uncertain. He goes on to set out the official version of events, according to which Tilapia was detained for blocking the movement of a fuel tanker, and Barberan was arrested when he intervened to defend Tilapia. The workers are dumbfounded by this outrageous fabrication. Then one screams: "That's a lie!" and a cacophony of voices seek to set the record straight. Tilapia had not obstructed a fuel tanker – he had been seized while he was walking down the street. And Barberan had not sought to prevent Tilapia's arrest – he wasn't even present when Tilapia was arrested, and he had been detained in a completely different place. Neither of them had been "caught red handed," and the police were acting on the orders of the company.[3]

Gallegos listens to their testimonies, then turns back to the bureaucrat. "So, who gave the order?" he repeats. The bureaucrat composes himself and responds with the same condescension with which he had previously addressed the Indigenous workers: "My little priest (*Padrecito*)," he begins, "Excuse me for explaining things in such simplistic terms, but if the police see someone committing a crime in front of them then they are obliged to act." Gallegos fixes him with a beady glare: "What crime were they committing?" The bureaucrat knows he cannot repeat the same lie at this point without risking being lynched on the spot. "If the police have taken action, then they must have done *something* wrong," he mumbles with a weak shrug of his rounded shoulders. "I see," Gallegos says with undisguised disdain, "Now you tell me: What right does the government have to detain people who are freely exercising their right to resistance?" The bureaucrat splutters a few incoherent syllables, but Gallegos cuts him off:

> You have to tell the army to withdraw, because its presence is intimidating. What happens if some idiot throws a stone? They'll launch their teargas, and everything will go to hell, and it will be a repeat of what happened here ten years ago.[4]

But the bureaucrat is back on script: "Both the military and the police are exercising their proper functions," he says curtly. Like the workers before him, the priest has rapidly reached the limits of his tolerance for this infuriating little upstart. "Look mate," he growls, "I've lived in the Amazon for forty-five years, and it's always been the same story. The people fight for their rights, and the security forces repress them." But such perspectives cannot be computed by the bureaucratic brain. "I was sent here to inform you about legal matters," the bureaucrat repeats. "If you have any concerns in this regard, I am here to respond to them. Anything else is beyond my remit." "Yes. Thank you very much," Gallegos concludes sarcastically, "But these people are going to keep demanding their rights."

*****

While this debate is going on, the soldiers descend from the top of the hill and close in behind us. They approach slowly, swinging their nightsticks and teargas launchers with an attitude of nonchalant aggression. Some of them are wearing balaclavas under their helmets to conceal their identity. There is a sense that things are about to kick off. Gallegos warns me to stop taking photographs if I want to avoid arrest. We fall back to our position in front of the gates, and the standoff is resumed. The priest and the colonel become locked in a heated conversation in the space between the battle lines, too far away to be heard. Whatever Gallegos says, it works. As night falls, the soldiers retreat again to the top of the hill, silhouetted against the last light of the evening sky.

Soon afterwards people begin to drift away from the *paro*, leaving a hard core of 30 or 40 workers who will camp out overnight – "dawning" (*amaneciendo*), as they call it. Everyone is surprised to have survived this long. If Correa had still been president, they say, the crackdown would already have taken place. But Lenín Moreno's political strategy is based on distancing himself from Correa's legacy in every respect. This means abandoning twenty-first century socialism in favor of neoliberal reforms – a move that is unlikely to be popular in itself. But this shift has been legitimated by a symbolic rejection of the ugliest dimensions of the Correa regime – corruption and the repression of resistance. Correa began his presidency with the militarized crushing of a *paro* in Dayuma. If Moreno is trying to frame himself as the "anti-Correa," then he won't want to begin his term of office in exactly the same way. But on the other hand, there is only so long that he can allow a popular insurrection against a transnational corporation to continue, if he is going to convince foreign capital that Ecuador has returned to the overtly "market friendly" policies of the past.

The general consensus is that the military will return to remove them in the morning. I tell those who are "dawning" that I will be there before sunrise and walk back to my hotel, where I send a flood of emails to my contacts in Quito, hoping to be able to get the story out. I have promised the workers that I will publicize their struggle. This is what I have to offer as a contribution to the *paro*, and as proof that I am truly fighting on their side. After all, who the fuck *am* I? Some random gringo academic, who just happened to show up at the start of the first uprising to have taken place in these parts in a decade? It's not a very plausible story, even though it happens to be true. I arrived with the – admittedly somewhat grudging – approval of the legendary rebel leader Jhon Rosero. But even so, there are sure to be those who suspect me of being a spy working for the government, or the company, or both. I send the last email and try to catch some sleep.

*****

I get back to the frontline around 5am, as the first light gleams on the forested horizon. Someone passes me a plastic cup of aguardiente "for the cold," although the night feels pretty warm to me. Everyone is awake and awaiting the first sign of movement from the army encamped at the top of the hill. But nothing happens. The first busloads of workers usually start rolling in here by 6am, ready for a

6:30 start. But the company buses are locked inside the camp behind us, which is empty now apart from the security guards. Instead, a public bus passes through heading south, and 20 or 30 people get off to join the *paro*. Others gradually arrive by motorbike and on foot. Some of them gather around an older worker with reading glasses perched on the tip of his nose, who haltingly reads out chunks of labor legislation and extracts from the constitution by the light of a mobile phone. Others stand around in small groups, talking in low voices in the gathering light.

Before long the sky darkens again, and at 7am we are struck by a torrential rainstorm. A huge sheet of black plastic is dragged out of a nearby construction site and propped up with planks and branches from the river, to form an impromptu marquee under which we all take shelter. People pull up logs and concrete blocks to use as seats, while others lounge across the oil pipelines that run along the roadside. A Colombian woman who usually hawks 20-cent cups of coffee to workers entering the *Obrador Central* has set up shop under the tent and is doing a brisk trade.

At 9am or so, a large group of *Shuar* from the *comuna* of Charapa join the *paro*. They are led by Bolívar Naichap, the president of the community and the father of Olger Naichap – the young *Shuar* worker who had confronted the pedantic bureaucrat the day before. They arrive not in the oil company uniforms that Olger and several others had been wearing the previous day, but in full ceremonial dress armed with long wooden spears, their faces etched with the red ink of the *achiote* seed. Bolívar is greeted by Santiago Jempekta, another *Shuar* leader, who has been at the forefront of the struggle of the local unemployed to be given work with CGA. Now all three components of the original sit-down strike are present in force: workers, Indigenous communities, and the unemployed. The rain has stopped, the sun is out, and the two leaders launch into a "*Saludo Shuar*" – the dance that is traditionally performed between the leaders of *Shuar* communities when they unite to confront a shared adversary. They rush at each other repeatedly, thrusting their spears just past each other's heads and shouting "*Jestei! Jestei!*" The message is not of aggression but solidarity. As an elderly *Shuar* woman explains: "*Jestei* means 'Be brave, don't chicken out [*no se acobarden*]!' That's how our ancestors supported our struggles in the past. *Jestei!* It's a form of support that says: 'Everyone united!'"

Meanwhile the *Shuar* on the sidelines shout slogans of support for the *paro*, raising their spears into the air with each defiant exclamation. Soon the mestizo workers join in the chanting, which underpins the cries of the two leaders and adds further drama to their fight: "*Viva el paro!*" – "*Viva!*" "*Viva Dayuma!*" – "*Viva!*" "*Viva el pueblo Shuar!*" – "*Viva!*" "*Get out CGA!*" – "*Get out!*" A police contingent approaches from behind the military lines, and Bolívar and Santiago conclude their dance and climb the hill to confront them. They are accompanied by the women of Charapa in bright red dresses, and a group of mestizo workers, some of whom are now carrying *Shuar* spears. Santiago does not wait for the cops to set the terms of the debate. Instead, he informs them that he and Bolívar are not only speaking on behalf of the *Shuar*, but for "*Shuar*, *colono*, *Huaorani* and *Kichwa*," all of whom are united in the *paro*.

Bolívar now addresses the police:

> We have launched this struggle because we ran out of other options. We have no alternative ... We will not block the road, we will not block the bridges, we will not seize the camp. We are only asking for the liberation of our two companions and to come to an agreement with the company.

The chief of police of Orellana responds by telling Bolívar that the *Shuar* must disarm by laying down their spears. But Bolívar rejects this outright, bluntly informing him that "This is our culture." Of equal importance, the spears are the only weapons that this motley crew possesses in its standoff with the army. In fact, this is central to their cultural significance, as the same elderly *Shuar* woman later points out: "In the *paros* we always carry spears, because our ancestors also defended themselves with spears. Now we likewise need to use the spear."[5]

The chief of police reluctantly consents. They can remain here for now, bearing their spears, as long as they don't block the road. Meanwhile, he will report back to the governor. The *paro* has received another stay of execution. A delegation is dispatched to the parish council building, to seek the support of Judith Hidalgo. The rest of us await further developments, sheltering from the sun beneath the black tarpaulin. The *Shuar* of Kapáku have arrived, led by the president of the *comuna*, Marco Kapáku. They pass the time by telling the story of their kidnap of Esteban García, to the great amusement of everyone. Like the rest of the Argentinian managers of CGA, García had subjected the *Shuar* to months of exploitation, humiliation, and racist abuse, and he had been laughing at the detention of their companions just before they seized him. "Laugh now!" they told him, after they had thrown him in the back of the truck. But he just huddled in the corner, muttering a little prayer to himself. He needn't have worried. They had no intention of doing him any real harm. They just wanted to apply a bit of "Indigenous justice" (*justicia indígena*), and a very mild form of it at that. They were going to strip him naked and whip him with nettles, which is what they do to punish spoiled children. Then they were going to rub hot chili in his eyes, which is what they do to the children who don't learn their lesson with the nettles. And finally, as a special treat just for him, they were going to shove a load of extra-hot chilies right up his racist ass.

"It was going to be a party," one of the Kapáku clan says wistfully. But then the cops blocked the road and spoiled the fun. Before they released García, they had struck a deal with him in the back of the truck. One of them had filmed it on their phone, and now everyone crowds around to try to get a look. García is squeezed in the back seat, between two *Shuar* women, and is gazing with puppy-dog eyes at the *indígenas* he had previously denigrated. He is being interrogated by a *Shuar* man, who remains off camera. The man is demanding that García guarantee the release of Tilapia in return for his own freedom (they were not aware of Barberan's detention at the time.) "Are you going to let me sleep in my own room?" García whimpers in response. "If he can also sleep in his own room," comes the stern reply. "OK," says García meekly. He is biting his lip and blinking back the tears. "If you break your word, there will be serious consequences," says the man. Then they throw García out of the truck onto the Savage Road.

As they are telling the story for the third or fourth time, the delegation returns from their meeting with Judith Hidalgo. The parish council is sympathetic with the complaints and objectives of the *paro*. But it cannot support it officially. Unlike previous *paros* in Dayuma, this one lacks the widespread backing of the town. The boom generated by CGA's arrival in Block 61 has created a local class of commercial traders and restaurant and hotel owners who are making healthy profits from the presence of the company. And most of the higher skilled and better paid workers – many of whom come from other parts of the country – are not members of the *comité* and are keeping their distance from the *paro*. Like the local bourgeoisie, they have a vested interest in the status quo.

The *paro* is therefore almost entirely composed of unskilled workers and the unemployed (along with their family members and other marginalized inhabitants of Dayuma and nearby communities). The main exceptions to this rule are the leading representatives of the *comité*, most of whom have a relatively high level of formal education and hold relatively well-paid positions in the company. These leaders are not on the street but hiding out in a makeshift headquarters cut into the steep slope that runs below the roadside behind the black plastic marquee. If they were on the frontline, they would be vulnerable to the same fate that befell Tilapia and Barberan yesterday. Instead, they are organizing things from behind the scenes, while the *Shuar* leaders take charge of the *paro* itself, with Olger Naichap, who is both a *Shuar* leader and a representative of the *comité*, working as the hinge between the two. I become aware of this division of labor when searching for a spokesperson to give an interview to *Bloomberg*'s representative in Ecuador, who has responded to one of my emails and has given me a call. At this point, the distrust with which I am viewed by some of those involved in the *paro* becomes clear. I am not allowed to meet with the leaders. Instead, my phone is taken from me and delivered to their clandestine HQ, while I am made to wait on the road until the interview has concluded and my phone is returned, on the understanding that I will publish something soon.

*****

In the afternoon, the pedantic bureaucrat returns to announce that the governor has been in discussions with CGA, who have agreed to open negotiations to bring the *paro* to an end. They will be held behind closed doors tomorrow morning in the governor's offices in Coca, and will be attended by delegations from the government, the company and the *paro*, along with the presidents of the four parish councils of the region. The proposal is positively received by the *paro*. But they insist that the negotiations must be held in public in Dayuma, not behind closed doors in Coca. They are wise to this trick. It is a tactic of oil companies and the government that is all too familiar from previous struggles: negotiate in private with a group of leaders, pay them off, and then get them to use their influence to bring the *paro* to an end without granting any substantive concessions.

The bureaucrat is sent away with his tail between his legs. Soon after he has departed, Gonzalo Plazarte appears – the Afro-descendant leader of countless *paros* in the 1990s and 2000s, who had been inspired by the radio transmissions of the FARC while working on his family *finca*. Plazarte ranks alongside Jhon Rosero as one of the most legendary figures of the golden age of the *paros*. But following the military crackdown in 2007, he switched sides and joined Correa's party, Alianza PAIS, before being elected president of the parish council, which he ran from 2010 to 2014. He now has a successful business providing mechanical services to the oil industry, and he still maintains a close relationship with the governor.

Plazarte pulls up on a high-powered motorbike, with a much younger woman in a very short skirt riding on the back. He has put on weight since his street-fighting days, and his belly spills over his belt from behind his open floral shirt. But he still has the magnetism of a natural leader. He launches into an impassioned speech in defense of the *paro*, followed by a summary of his role in previous struggles. Soon he has everyone's rapt attention. Then he repeats the same message that was just delivered by the bureaucrat: "The governor says that the negotiations must be in Coca." This provokes the same forthright rejection from the crowd, though in far more respectful terms than those with which the pedantic bureaucrat has just been dispatched. Plazarte nods in thoughtful agreement. Then he reaches into his pocket and produces an unusually large and shiny smartphone. He tells the crowd that he will now call the governor to inform him of their decision. With a conspiratorial wink, he adds that he will secretly put the governor on speakerphone, so that the crowd can hear his response. Everyone is spellbound, craning forward to hear the voice of the governor, while Plazarte signals to them to keep quiet so as not to give the game away.

Remarkably, the governor picks up after just one ring, and explains in a confidential tone that the meeting must be held in Coca, as there will be high-ranking ministers flying in from Quito. Their presence at the negotiations shows how seriously the government is taking the situation. But they have made special room for this in their very tight agendas, and they simply don't have time to come all the way to Dayuma. "OK nice one mate! (*Listo mi pana!*)" says Plazarte to the governor. "Yep, that's it. Thanks. See you later." He slides his enormous phone back into his pocket. Everyone is suitably impressed with his high connections and his willingness to put them to use in the defense of the people. And as they have just heard from the horse's mouth, there really is no other option than to hold the negotiations in Coca. This time, the crowd grants its consent. Plazarte kicks his bike into life and speeds away, to cries of "*Gracias Gonzalo!*" Job done.

Soon after his departure, the *paro* is treated to another surreal blast from the past. It's getting dark, and I'm milling around with the rest of the crowd, talking with people as they prepare for another "dawning." As I do so, I keep catching glimpses of a man shooting me dirty looks from the side of the road. He is dressed in a shirt and chinos, clutching a briefcase, and standing with a group of cops and low-level government functionaries, who are quietly scrutinizing the crowd. There is something weirdly familiar about the guy. Then he calls for the crowd's attention and begins to deliver a speech on behalf of the governor, and with a sinking feeling in my stomach I recognize him as Wilmer Armas. It scarcely seems possible. Wilmer Armas was the vice-president of the parish council, Jhon Rosero's second in command, at the time of the *paro* of 2007. He's the one the soldiers seized at the barricade – the one they beat the shit out of and doused in teargas before turning on the rest of the town. I recognize him from a photograph taken at the scene, in which a group of soldiers is leading him toward the truck in which he is going to receive his beating. He is wearing the rubber boots and threadbare clothes of a typical *colono*, and his wide eyes show that he knows what is coming.

Wilmer Armas spent a long time in a very rough prison after that. And yet, like Gonzalo Plazarte, he ended up siding with his persecutors. Not long after he got out of jail, he shifted his allegiance from Pachakutik to Alianza PAIS, and was elected as rural councilor of the municipality of Coca, which is closely allied with the governor. He has traded his *colono* outfit for a shirt and trousers and has swapped the traumas of resistance for the trappings of minor office. Now he is standing just a few feet away from where his beating took place a decade ago and is defending the regime that administered it to him.

He has come to inform the *paro* of the good work that the governor has been doing on their behalf: "Our esteemed governor went so far as to meet with the president of the Republic and various ministers today," he declares, "and they immediately resolved to send a delegation." The line is delivered with an obsequious smile. But he lacks the rebel pedigree and political charisma of Plazarte, and there are immediate mutterings of dissent in the crowd. Armas plows on regardless, explaining that tomorrow's negotiations in Coca will be attended by representatives of the Labor Ministry, the Ministry of Hydrocarbons, and the Ministry of the Interior. The *paro* should carefully select their own delegation, he says, and they must act "in peace and harmony" throughout the negotiations. The sanctimonious tone of this last remark is met with shouts of derision, and someone accuses him of treachery. "*Por favor compañero*," Armas responds in a wounded voice, "I speak with the greatest sincerity. I was an oil worker just like you and I am totally in agreement with your struggle. I would never take the side of the company. I could never betray you."

This last remark draws a smattering of applause, after which someone in the crowd comes to his defense: "A long time ago we were *compañeros* in prison. He was also a delinquent like me!" Everyone laughs at this, and the man continues: "Why was he in prison? To defend our rights as we are doing today. And what did they do to us? They bombarded us with teargas from helicopters! That's why I say 'Dayuma never submits!'" This is met with roars of "*Viva el pueblo!*" and "CGA get out!" Armas is off the hook, and he scuttles away, having discharged his little duty for the governor.

These are the miniature rituals through which power seeks to maintain its footing in volatile situations at the farthest reaches of the state, when insurgent universality begins to stir: the careful staging of authority performed with minimal props by soldiers, cops, and bureaucrats, and perplexing smoke-and-mirror acts in which the existing order is subtly defended in the name of the people by the old heroes of the resistance. But any consent gained is only ever provisional, and rage is only ever one wrong step from being relit.

*****

Suddenly the news arrives: the prisoners have been released and are returning to the *paro*! The celebrations are led by Bolívar Naichap, who instructs all men to strip off their shirts and everyone to grab a spear. It is a call to embody the universal humanity that is unmistakably emerging in the face of the savagery of state and capital, in which particular identities are superseded by a shared commitment to a common struggle against seemingly impossible odds. This universal dimension was visible in the launch of the initial sit-down strike by workers, Indigenous communities and the unemployed; in the kidnap of the company boss by *indígenas* to avenge the seizure of their mestizo comrades by the cops; in the making of speeches and bearing of banners defending Indigenous rights by mestizo workers; in the insistence of the *Shuar* leaders that they are representing not only their own group but everyone; in the solidarity conveyed in both the *Shuar* battle cry and the slogans shouted by *Shuar* and mestizo voices in response; and now in this explicit expression of unity, symbolized by the same naked flesh and the same wooden spear. And far from erasing Indigenous identity beneath an exclusionary appeal to a homogenizing Eurocentric universalism, it is indigeneity itself that is being invoked as the universal category – and being invoked as such by the *indígenas* themselves: "Here we are all Indigenous!", Bolívar shouts with his spear raised high, "There is neither *Shuar*, nor *Kichwa*, nor *Huao*, nor mestizo!"

Soon both sides of the Savage Road are lined with women and men of all races and ethnicities wielding spears and chanting "*Viva el paro!*" at every vehicle that passes. Bolívar now calls on one man after another to take part in the same ritual that he performed with Santiago this morning. Each dance is more enthusiastic than the last, and each time the men holler the same *Shuar* ancestral call to unity and solidarity with even greater abandon: "*Jestei! Jestei!*" Huge chants go up around them as they dance: "*Viva el paro!*" "*Viva Dayuma!*" "*Viva los Shuar!*" Before long a bus arrives from Coca, and Barberan and Tilapia jump down into the throng. They are hoisted on the shoulders of the crowd and paraded around in triumph, punching their fists in the air. Then Barberan delivers a brief speech, in which the universality of the uprising is once again expressed: "They took us prisoner saying that we are the leaders [of the *paro*]. We were never the leaders. Who are the leaders here?" The crowd responds in unison: "Everyone! Everyone!"

The release of the prisoners is now celebrated with a "caravan of struggle (*caravana de lucha*)." We pile into the backs of three beat-up old pickup trucks and head up the hill into town, with others riding motorbikes and running along the roadside. Everyone is shouting, honking horns, bashing pots and pans, stomping feet and clapping hands, clashing their spears against each other and slapping the sides of the trucks in a cacophonous rebel symphony: "Unite yourself with the people! Unite yourself with the people!" Figures gather in shopfronts and doorways, on balconies and street corners. But then do not join us. Instead, they watch in silence, as the caravan of struggle winds its way through every street in town, the cries to unify repeated with undiminished intensity.

As we return to the company gates, a woman leaps down from the truck and embraces me, and I recognize her as Rosa Kapáku, the *Shuar* woman wearing the "Wild Style" shirt in the photograph of the kidnap of Esteban García. Her eyes are shining. "That's how a *caravana de lucha* should be!" she laughs. Then Barberan comes over and slaps me on the back. "It's so exciting to live it! (*Esto es bien emocionante vivirlo!*)" he says as the celebrations spiral around us There is an uncannily ecstatic atmosphere, born of stark circumstances and desperate action, and surging upward in a chaotic whirlwind of collective egalitarian passion. No one seems to care that the people in town have ignored their invitation to join the *paro*. Everyone is elated by the achievements of the day. Their comrades have been released, and they have forced the company and the government to the negotiating table. The night is clear, the stars are blazing, and by this time tomorrow their victory is sure to be complete.

5 Battling a Monster

By 8am the sun is rampant and the *paro* is in full swing. The delegation is preparing to depart for the negotiations in Coca, and they must be given a good send-off. Olger Naichap opens proceedings by repeating his father's universalist message of the night before, in the words reported at the beginning of this book: "We are going to paint ourselves because we are all Indigenous! Now everyone, raise your spears and shout: '*Viva el paro!*'"

The delegation includes Judith Hidalgo and Jhon Rosero from the parish council, the *Shuar* leaders Bolívar Naichap, Marco Kapáku, and Santiago Jempekta, and the two principal representatives of the *comité*, who now emerge from their clandestine headquarters for the first time: the general secretary, Darío Rodríguez – a tall Afro-descendant from the coast, and the treasurer, Manuel Méndez – a stocky mestizo from the highlands. They are dispatched with a barrage of slogans from Edison Kapáku – the *Shuar* man who made a statement to me alongside Barberan and Tilapia just before their arrest, and the brother of Marco, Linda, and Rosa, with whom he forms a formidable rebel family quartet: "Give it everything you've got *compañeros!*" he shouts as the vehicles depart. "Fear no-one! Only death has no solution! … We are the ones who will solve this! We are the bosses here!"

After the delegation has departed, the rest of us hunker down and await further news. Spirits are high at first. But as the hours pass, the tension mounts. The negotiations are being held behind closed doors, and no one knows what is taking place inside. This uncertainty is mixed with a growing sense of paranoia. Sleek SUVs with blacked-out windows keep cruising by. Everyone says they are *inteligencia* – spies from the Interior Ministry. A drone appears overhead, circling safely out of range of the stones flung in its direction. But the pilots are spotted in a patch of waste ground at the top of the hill. A gang of workers rev their motorbikes, and Edison tells me to go with them to record what happens. I leap on the back of one of the bikes and we fly up the hill – me clutching my notebook and recorder, the passengers of the other bikes all brandishing their spears. The pilot and his assistant would seem to have stumbled unawares into this scene. A couple of well-meaning middle-class guys from Quito on an assignment in the "land of beasts and savages." The pilot is neatly dressed, with a carefully clipped mustache, and his young assistant is wearing a T-shirt emblazoned with the name of an avant-garde Parisian electronica band. They stand rooted to the spot outside

DOI: 10.4324/9781003345879-5

their van as a dozen motorbikes filled with "savages" and bristling with spears come hurtling toward them across the waste ground like some kind of Mad Max jungle nightmare.

Within seconds they are surrounded, and the spears are pointed at their heads. The older man clutches at my shirt, apparently assuming that the only white person in attendance is the only hope he's got: "Help me!" he chokes in desperation. I suggest that he land the drone as rapidly as possible. He turns his face to the sky and begins scrabbling with the remote control, while pleading that that they know nothing of the *paro*, and are merely doing a cartographic survey for the municipality. He can't get the drone to follow his instructions, and he keeps glancing frantically over his shoulder at the spear that Linda Kapáku is holding impatiently against his back. Meanwhile his assistant is searching through his files, trying to find their contract with the municipal government, all the while babbling about his hatred of the oil industry, which he wrongly assumes that the *paro* is opposing. Accustomed to seeing the Amazon through the romantic colonial lens of jungle tours and Hollywood movies like James Cameron's *Avatar*, it is inconceivable to nice middle-class liberals from Quito – or indeed from Europe or the USA – that the Indigenous inhabitants of the region might be fighting for their rights as workers in the oil industry, rather than defending nature against its depredations.

"My girlfriend is an activist, she hates oil!" the young man in the painfully cool T-shirt stammers eagerly. The men around him have their shirts wrapped around their faces to conceal their identities, but they do not appear to be impressed by his protestations. As a last-ditch attempt to save his skin he offers to fly spy missions for them over the *Obrador Central*. Meanwhile the pilot has finally managed to land the drone, which is mounted with a camera. The masked men turn away from his assistant without commenting on his offer, and supervise the pilot while he wipes the camera's memory. They call the municipal government in Coca to check the story, and who should respond but Wilmer Armas, who scolds them for their actions, and assures them that this is a legitimate cartography project. But as they point out afterwards, it is peculiar timing for such a project to be undertaken in the middle of a *paro*. Whatever. The camera has been cleared and the terrified cartographers are released. We watch their van rush gratefully away across the wasteland. "That was a game," says Pedro – the pug-faced guy with the mohawk. Not necessarily a spy mission. Maybe just a bit of head-fuckery to add to the paranoia of those involved in the *paro*, and probably without the knowledge of the unfortunate cartographers who are now thanking their lucky stars.

But the eyes of the enemy are everywhere. Even – and perhaps especially – among ourselves. We are sheltering from the sun beneath the black tarpaulin, when Pedro slowly gets to his feet and ambles over to where two unfamiliar men are sitting. "Get out," he says in a soft voice, barely above a whisper. He is standing over them, and casually sharpening his spear with a shard of broken glass. They say they are just here to check out what is going on. "Get out," he repeats with a curl of his lip, raking the glass up and down the tip of his spear. They leave without another word.

Lunch arrives and we all queue up to receive a polystyrene box of chicken and rice and a plastic bag of sugary juice. This is one of the things the *comité* is organizing behind the scenes. The *paro* is provided with three free meals a day, all prepared with donated food and cooked in nearby homes. And every once in a while, someone shows up with a truckload of something extra – mandarins, watermelons, or vats of coffee. As we are eating, Pedro tells me about the two guys he threw out. They were "toads (*sapos*)" he says – informants working for the company or the cops, or both. They are the ones who provide the real information. The drone and the blacked-out SUVs are just cynical ways of ratcheting up the bad vibes.[1]

In this context, I am regarded with increased suspicion. After lunch, one of the leaders of the *comité* takes me to one side. He wants to know when I'm going to publish something on the *paro* as I had promised. "It's been days now," he hisses. "You say you are reporting, but there are no results." He's got a point. The *Bloomberg* interview has come to nothing, and I've been circulating a press release that no one has picked up. I try to explain this and promise to redouble my efforts. I ask his name, so that I can locate him as soon as I have any news. But he turns his back and walks away.

The day drags on, and the mood continues to darken. Then at around 4:30pm, Edison Kapáku receives a call from his brother Marco, who has just emerged from the negotiations. He listens in silence, straining to catch his brother's words on his battered old cellphone. Then he hangs up, and it is clear from his face that the news is not good. "Nothing has been agreed!" he shouts, "And why haven't they found a solution? Because the representatives of CGA didn't show up!" The only people in attendance, it turns out, were the governor, their own delegation, and a couple of local functionaries from the oil and labor ministries – the delegation of ministers who were supposed to have been dispatched from Quito by the Ecuadorian president hadn't shown up either.

Everyone had expected the company and the ministers to drive a hard bargain in the negotiations. But no one had foreseen that they would not even bother to participate. This was an act of calculated arrogance and deliberate humiliation – a clear refusal to recognize the participants in the *paro* as legitimate interlocutors with grievances that could be expressed in rational debate. In their absence, the negotiations had effectively been between the delegation from the *paro* and the governor, with the governor unambiguously representing the interests of the company.

Everyone is outraged. But in contrast to the exuberant belligerence of previous days, the atmosphere is deflated, the energy leaking out like air from a punctured tire. Yesterday, Gonzalo Plazarte and Wilmer Armas had assured them that the governor was on their side. But this is clearly not the case. "The governor has been bought off by the company," says one renegade. "He took a big bribe and now they've told him this is his problem to sort out," says another. "The Labor Ministry must have been bought off too," mutters a third, "That's how [the company] can get away without paying *utilidades*. They've bought off all the politicians and now they can do whatever they like."

The delegation soon returns from Coca, and Judith Hidalgo informs us that the negotiations have been rescheduled for Tuesday, September 5. This time, the governor has provided them with written assurance that the negotiations will take place in Dayuma, with CGA and the relevant ministers present. But Tuesday is six days away. In the meantime, the governor is demanding that the workers suspend the *paro* and return to work. The strategy is now clear: raise false hopes about today's negotiations, which were presumably never going to happen. Then shatter these hopes, and break what remains of the workers' will by scheduling the next set of negotiations far enough in the future that the continuation of the *paro* becomes unsustainable. After all, six days is a long time for impoverished people in desperate need of the meager salary that the company provides. The workers and their unemployed comrades listen to the news in silence, their eyes turned to the ground. The egalitarian passion of the uprising has abruptly receded to reveal the poverty and humiliation of an exploited and abandoned population, confronted with the undiminished power of state and capital, and the unaltered severity of the conditions that forced them to take this action in the first place.

Then Edison Kapáku looks up, and steps into the circle in the middle of the crowd:

> *Compañeros*, we are going to make more spears! In preparation for Tuesday! We're going to make two hundred, three hundred, as many spears as we need *compañeros*! Because this battle is against a monster! And this monster must be crushed! No-one fucks with Dayuma! The oil is here. And [the oil companies] are benefitting from money that is ours. So, if we need to spill blood here, then we will spill blood here *compañeros*! I fear no-one! If I have to die, I will die! But I will do so for my rights, and for the rights of my children, and for the rights of all the children who exist here. *Compañeros*, we are going to fight on! We are going to stay here until Tuesday, exactly as we are! *Compañeros* we must unite! Everyone must unite!

These words burn through the pall of despondency that had settled on the crowd and reignite the rage that lay smoldering beneath. Once again, the air booms with huge cries of "*Viva Dayuma!*" and "*Viva el paro!*" The decision is immediate and unanimous: the *paro* will be maintained until the negotiations on Tuesday. The governor's strategy has failed, and CGA remains under lockdown.

*****

Dayuma is a ghost town on a knife edge. The battle lines have been redrawn, and now each side is digging in and plotting its next move. The engineers and managers employed by CGA and their subcontractors have all been sent home until further notice, and the hotels and bars stand empty. On the morning of the fourth day of the *paro*, the woman cleaning my room tells me that the Hotel Guerrero has 64 rooms and has been full for months. Now it's just me and a couple of guys who rent rooms on a permanent basis. I eat breakfast alone in a cavernous restaurant designed for legions of oil workers. "There's usually a lot of movement at this hour," says the waitress, "But now the whole town has been abandoned. There's something heavy in the air (*es un ambiente pesado*)."

She's right. I can feel it when I walk through town, on my way back and forth between my hotel room and the *paro*. There is a palpable sense of antipathy in the silence of the mechanics and shop owners who watch me pass. While I may still be regarded with suspicion by some of those involved in the *paro*, it's perfectly clear to everyone else whose side I'm on, and they don't like it. But no one says anything. Then, as I am having lunch in another empty restaurant, a local businessman approaches me and snarls into my ear: "We are opposed to the *paro!*" I look around. He is breathing heavily, and dark patches of sweat have broken through his light blue shirt. He says that the *paro* is just the selfish action of a handful of greedy people who are ruining the legitimate businesses of everyone else. The restaurant owner sits with her arms folded on the far side of the room, nodding slowly and staring at me without a word. It is not racial or cultural identity but class antagonism – with the enemy ranging from multinational capital right down to the pettiest local bourgeoisie – along which the battle lines of this struggle are being drawn.

Returning to my hotel room after lunch, I find that an article based on my press release has at last appeared online. I print off 30 copies and distribute them at the blockade. But the leader who questioned me about this yesterday is nowhere to be found. In fact, the *paro* is notably sparser than on previous days. Many of the striking workers are beginning to slack off, relying on the hardcore to hold the fort until Tuesday, while they work on their *fincas*. This leaves the *paro* vulnerable to a sudden army-led eviction. To counter this, the *comité* announces a policy designed to keep everyone on board. Starting from now, an attendance register will be taken every day. Those employees of CGA with full attendance will be guaranteed to keep their jobs after the *paro*. But those who are absent will be replaced by the unemployed workers who are registered as having participated in the struggle, and this will be one of the principles insisted upon in the negotiations.

The measure proves effective, and the *paro* grows steadily in number over the following days. But the company has a new tactic of its own. On the morning of the fifth day of the *paro*, I arrive to find the place in uproar. A countermovement has emerged – literally overnight. It includes local business owners and workers not involved in the *comité*. Messages have been circulating on social media, presenting the *paro* as a bunch of lazy delinquents, and including racist insults against the Indigenous contingent. Everyone opposed to the *paro* is being invited to a rally, to be held at 10am in the "coliseum" in Dayuma. The movement has been organized by Fernando Charango and Jonathan Chimbo, two CGA employees with close ties to the company management. At the time of the formation of the *comité* a few months ago, elections were held among the workers to select its leadership. Chimbo and Charango had put themselves forward, with the full support of CGA, but had been roundly defeated.[2] Now they were bent on taking their revenge. One of the leaders of the *paro* shows me a short clip of Charango on his phone: a wiry mestizo in CGA uniform is standing in the Auca Central oil station, his face twisted with hatred: "We declare a civil war! They have spears, so we will arm ourselves with machetes, sticks, stones, whatever we can lay our hands on!"

This is a troubling turn of events. Confronted with the endurance of the *paro* following the betrayal of the negotiations, the company has evidently decided to intensify local tensions with the hope of provoking a violent confrontation. And the fact that Charango's threat was filmed in the facilities of the state oil company suggests that this plot is being executed with the knowledge and support of the government. This suspicion is strengthened by the arrival of three armored personnel carriers. The *paro* falls silent as we watch them roll past, heading in the direction of the coliseum.

Once again, it is Edison Kapáku who intervenes to raise the spirits of the crowd. "Charango is a criminal! Whoever comes here for a fight will get what they are looking for!" he yells into the cloud of dust raised by the roaring trucks. Then he turns to address his comrades. The people involved in the countermovement have sold out to the company, he says. They are defending the interests of the wealthy – the company managers and the venal politicians who run the national oil industry:

> They all have their beautiful houses! Their beautiful gardens! Their beautiful "mansions," as they call them! Who among you has a mansion? Who among you has anything at all *compañeros*? What can a worker do with $380 [a month]? What can he buy? How is he going to afford shoes for his children? How is he going to pay for their education? *Compañeros*, we must win! … Call your families, call your friends, get them to join us! It is time to say "Enough!" No more slavery! No more marginalization!

He concludes by referring to the article that I had finally managed to publish about the *paro*. It was posted in a random section of an obscure website, but this is overlooked in the heat of the moment:

> Our struggle is being publicized at an international scale *compañeros*! News of this *paro* is reaching every corner of the country, every corner of the world *compañeros*! Because we are battling a monster! The same monster that has been stomping on people all around the world forever!

This is the second time that Edison has used the monster metaphor, and now he is starting to flesh it out, presenting multinational companies, corrupt politicians, and complicit workers as integrated elements of a single monstrous system operating on a global scale. A few minutes after he has finished his speech, news arrives that the meeting of the countermovement is underway. His militant sister Rosa Kapáku immediately calls on everyone to storm the coliseum "with our spears." But in contrast to his bellicose attitude of a few minutes earlier, Edison now insists that violence should be avoided if possible. Rosa should lead a delegation of *Shuar* women to confront the countermovement, with a small contingent of armed men backing them up from a distance. He asks me to accompany them to document the events. I climb into the back of the pickup with the women, and we speed up the hill toward the coliseum, followed by a dozen or so motorbikes of men. The women are tense and silent, knowing that things are about to get nasty. Rosa is wearing her Wild Style shirt again. And like her brother Edison, she is proving to be a natural leader in such situations: "We must not be afraid," she tells the others, "Let's arrive shouting 'The people united will never be defeated!'"

We roar into the parking lot and charge into the coliseum. But what we find is not the massive popular mobilization that we had feared. The "countermovement," it turns out, amounts to fewer than 50 people. The meeting is being filmed by the local cable news station, presumably to promote its cause to the rest of the region, and footage broadcast that evening shows the scene immediately prior to our arrival. In the footage, Colon Malla, the governor of Orellana, can be seen addressing the so-called countermovement, and denouncing the *paro* as "unjustified, given that negotiations have been organized to resolve the situation."[3] But in contrast to the angry messages that they supposedly posted on social media, most of his audience are paying little attention. Some are yawning, and others are idly swiping their smartphones. They are notably whiter and more affluent than the participants in the *paro*. Apart from a few local business owners, they are higher salaried workers from other parts of the country, who the participants in the *paro* say were probably paid to be here, and who must have been smuggled in on those armored personnel carriers along with the governor.

They aren't scrolling through their Facebook pages anymore. They are cowering on their concrete seats, as a gang of spear-wielding Indigenous women rushes furiously toward them. Colon Malla has disappeared, and Chimbo and Charango are nowhere to be found. But someone else has been caught with his pants down: Wilmer Armas, the minor rebel leader who was beaten and imprisoned during the military crackdown in 2007, and subsequently joined the government. He has always insisted that he did so to better defend the interests of the people. OK, so what the hell is he doing here? The *Shuar* women veer away from their confrontation with the countermovement, and head toward Armas, who is backed up by a group of cops. Rosa takes the lead, and she is apoplectic:

"You are working very badly sir!" she begins, with admirable restraint. "No" says Armas flatly, in the absence of a plausible excuse. He is sneering and squirming as Rosa closes in: "You were elected by the people to support the people, not to betray the people!" The rest of the *Shuar* women crowd around them. "I represent everyone," Armas replies in his smug and mealy-mouthed manner, rocking back on his heels with his briefcase held before his crotch. "You are betraying the people Mister Councilor!" Rosa insists. Her voice is rising, and she is jabbing her finger ever closer to his smirking face. Then she turns her wrath upon the members of the phony countermovement, who remain slouched on the grandstand, rolling their eyes and trying to conceal their terror beneath an unconvincing attitude of nonchalant disdain: "[You] need to leave right now because the rest of us are on our way here, and we don't want any problems!" She is gesticulating fiercely and shouting at the top of her voice, backed by the other women: "We will not retreat a single step! I have taken my stand as a warrior woman (*mujer luchadora*)! This is what my mother and father raised me to do!"

Now Rosa wheels back toward the hapless Wilmer Armas. She wants to know why he didn't defend Tilapia and Barberan at the time of their detention, and why he hasn't shown his face at the *paro* since the night of their release. "I'm coming, I'm coming," Armas replies, trying and failing to affect an air of casual informality, "I'll just finish things up here and then I'll head right over." But Rosa has had enough: "I'm not going to listen to another word from you!" she screams with furious abandon, "Shut your little mouth! Get your things! And get out of here!"

At this point a convoy of motorbikes and pickups filled with men from the *paro* barrels into the parking lot and begins circling around in front of the open-sided coliseum. They are brandishing spears and revving engines, in a repeat of the "caravan of struggle" that was held to celebrate the release of the two leaders, when the *paro* was calling on the rest of the population to "unite with the people." But this demand for unity has now been replaced with an unambiguous threat of physical violence. We march out of the coliseum and the convoy heads back down the hill. Word soon comes that the countermovement has dispersed. Nothing is heard of it again – another failed gambit of state and capital. The *paro* continues with greater conviction, and the company is back to square one.

*****

The situation feels dangerous. The confrontation in the coliseum has further upped the stakes and entrenched the divisions in the town, and my alignment with the *paro* has become increasingly evident to everyone who opposes it. I need to secure my information before anything happens that could put it at risk. While the renegades return to the blockade, I sneak back to my hotel room to upload everything onto Dropbox – once it's there it will be safe. As I am doing so, I find another online article based on my press release. I print off several copies and take them with me back to the blockade.

The confrontation has intensified the militancy of the *paro*, and the attempt of the governor to generate divisions has had the unintended consequence of broadening its popular support. A group of workers from Dayuma who had previously kept their distance have heard about the phony countermovement and are now asking to be allowed to join the struggle. And two members of the *Huaorani* from further up the *Vía Auca* also arrive to offer their support. This is a significant moment, because when the *Huaorani* get involved in a conflict, they mean business. They've killed plenty of oil workers in the past, and they murdered two government functionaries just up the road from here as recently as 2014.[4] In the words of one worker: "When [the *Huaorani*] come to a *paro* they come for serious action … They can enter the *Obrador* [*Central*] and kill whoever they find there." The younger of the two *Huaorani* men delivers a brief speech, informing the *paro* that the *Huaorani* will arrive in force if the situation is not resolved on Tuesday. He is accompanied by a man who was born before the first contact between the *Huaorani* and the American missionaries. A veteran of many brutal battles with the oil companies in the not-so-distant past, the old man stands in silence, with a blue cataract shining like a jewel in one eye.

The blatant manipulations of the governor have also led Judith Hidalgo to at last abandon all pretense of neutrality and align herself firmly with the *paro*. She arrives with the parish council sound system, which she lends to the *paro* as a symbol of the council's support. Within minutes it is wired up, and Indigenous folksongs and mestizo cumbias are blasting across the jungle. The *Shuar* throw on their ceremonial dress and launch into a series of impassioned dances. First men, then women, then children, then men and women together, and finally everyone. The same beautiful *Shuar* song is repeated again and again, both mournful and uplifting, as they dance in radiant sunshine on the Savage Road, with all the weight of state and capital aligned against them.

The song is sung by a choir of *Shuar* women, and concerns the location of their culture in the world. But it does not speak of the rooting of a specific identity in an established territory. Instead, it addresses the historical displacement of the *Shuar* from the southern Amazon, and their arrival here when the road was first cut. And although its lyrics are in *Shuar*, and cannot be understood by many of the crowd, they resonate with the experience of alienation shared by other elements of this frontier proletariat drawn to the *Vía Auca* by similar processes of dispossession, exploitation, and impoverishment: "I wander far away in another land/ A land I have never known/ I am here, dancing to this music/ I have come from another land and now I am here." The song then shifts from the singular to the plural, from the particular to the universal, and from a sense of disorientation to an affirmation of uprooted existence: "Why are we here?/ Is this not our land?/ We, as nationalities, are here/ We are present."[5]

The only member of the *Shuar* who does not dance is Edison Kapáku. He never dances, and he never wears ceremonial dress. He is standing on the sidelines, wearing ill-fitting jeans and a baggy long-sleeved T-shirt adorned with the idols and incantations of a different culture – images of skyscrapers interspersed with words in English: "USA. New York. Original. Authentic." But his face is etched with *achiote* to symbolize the stripes and whiskers of the jaguar – a powerful animal in *Shuar* mythology, whose strength, courage, and ferocity are channeled by *Shuar* leaders in times of confrontation. Now, inspired by the emotion of the moment, he plugs in the microphone and begins to shout over the music: "We are revolutionaries like … like … *ay*, I've forgotten his name … Like Che Guevara!" The dance whirls on, and Edison keeps bellowing his fragmented aphorisms, his thickly distorted voice mingling with the delicate harmonies of the folksong: "Now is our moment!" "Now we are not like before!" "Now we are new!" "The revolution is here!" "The revolution has to happen *compañeros!*" The dancing intensifies, and the crowd around the dancers begins chanting responses to Edison's interjections, as the song starts up again: "Dayuma aloft!" – "*Arriba!*" "This dance asks for resolution … These children ask for peace, tranquility, and development for everyone … The people of Dayuma don't want snitches … We don't want crooks … We want a dignified life for everyone, *Si o no compañeros?*" – "*Si!*" "We are revolutionaries! … We are fierce! … We are united!"

Now is probably not the most auspicious moment for the state to attempt a further strategy of division. But when Edison finally pauses to catch his breath, a tall pale man in skinny jeans, black shirt, and dark glasses sidles over to him and whispers in his ear. Edison signals for the music to stop, before introducing the man to the crowd as a representative of the Hydrocarbons Ministry. He then respectfully informs him that everyone is waiting to hear his proposal, and that he has “all afternoon” to solve their problems, should he wish to do so. But that isn’t exactly what the man has in mind. He introduces himself as “Alex Nunes, Analyst in Socio-Political Conflict Management for Hydrocarbon Development.” The Oil Ministry is full of people like him, with postgraduate degrees in Sociology and Anthropology, and training in the most effective means of sowing discord and engendering co-optation. There are murmurs of distrust from the crowd, which intensify when he informs them that he has just been at the coliseum, where he claims to have been invited to hear the proposals of the countermovement – a movement that he surely had a hand in inventing. People demand to know what he has to offer. Alex Nunes gazes regretfully at the carefully scuffed boots protruding from beneath his skinny jeans. He could of course promise “lots of nice things,” as “*el compañero* Edison” suggests. But unfortunately, he explains, the illegality of their actions makes this impossible. He agrees with the spirit of their struggle, and congratulates the crowd “for this action that you have taken, which demonstrates that Dayuma will always be unified, which is important. Nevertheless” – he adds, straightening his back and assuming a strict, commanding tone – “now what is needed is for you all to return to work, because your actions are damaging the entire Ecuadorian state, including yourselves.”

Alex Nunes waits patiently for the incredulous uproar to die down. Turning to Edison, he then continues in a softer voice: “I am aware of the petition of Kapáku” he assures him with a complicit nod of the head, as if conducting a clandestine conversation out of earshot of the rest. This attempt to divide the *paro* is performed with all the subtlety of a B movie villain. But Edison snatches the microphone from his grasp and turns to face the crowd: “What we are demanding here is equality! Is that not so *compañeros*?” The crowd roars its affirmation, and Edison cranes his neck to meet the gaze of the man from the Oil Ministry, who looks down on him dispassionately from behind his dark glasses:

> That is what we want here! The case of the community of Kapáku against Petroamazonas (regarding compensation for the drilling of oil wells in their territory) – we will deal with that in our community at another time … What we want is equality … And if CGA does not want to solve the problem, then the *pueblo* will fight until CGA takes its things and gets out of here!”

This is met with a huge cheer, and Edison Kapáku now adopts an officious, bureaucratic tone, as if speaking through the sneering lips of the Analyst in Socio-Political Conflict Management himself:

> That is our proposal, *señor* Alex Nunes. If there is someone, some authority, who wishes to solve it, then please invite them to do so. We need authorities who take decisions. Not someone who tells stories with fancy words. Thank

> you for your presence, *señor* Alex Nunes. [But] we are going to keep struggling until Tuesday to find a solution. And if [no solution is found], then the *pueblos* of all four parishes are going to rise up! We are going to fight like hell, because now being crushed has come to an end! Now Dayuma is revolutionary!

The crowd explodes into chants of "*Viva el paro!*" as Edison shouts after the swiftly disappearing figure of Alex Nunes, whose skinny ass is already slinking away down the hill: "We aren't going to give up until we achieve our objectives! *Gracias!*"

The music resumes, but the carnival is soon interrupted by a sudden rainstorm, and everyone runs for cover beneath the black plastic tarpaulin, which is no longer big enough to hold the whole crowd. By now there must be at least three hundred people here – the highpoint of the *paro* since the initial uprising. Lunch has arrived, and there is a plate of rice and stewed beef and a plastic bag of sugary lime water for everyone. The road had been closed for at least an hour by the impromptu festivities, and now a constant stream of oil tankers is dragging itself up the hill in a cloud of diesel smoke, while Edison Kapáku shouts into the microphone over the growling engines: "There goes the money of Dayuma! There goes the money of Inés Arango! Do you see it? Look! It's hidden in that tanker!"

There is still no sign of Wilmer Armas, despite his earlier assurance that he was just on his way. Indeed, he never dares to show his face again. But not long after the rain has stopped, Gonzalo Plazarte makes another enigmatic appearance. He praises the *paro* for their fortitude and encourages them to look for practical solutions. Then he ceremoniously announces that Colon Malla, the governor of Orellana, is preparing to address them, and advises them to make the most of this great opportunity.

The governor arrives half an hour later, under heavy police guard. He is the stereotypical picture of a corrupt small-time politician: slicked-back hair, a double chin, a white shirt pulled across his sweaty paunch, and voluminous black trousers that look like they could easily fall down. It is the first time he has graced the *paro* with his presence. He has done everything he could think of to avoid this moment: He sent the pedantic bureaucrat. He sent Plazarte. He sent Armas. He sent the clueless cartographers. He organized a fake negotiation. He organized a phony countermovement with the help of Alex Nunes. And when all else failed, he sent Alex Nunes. But the *paro* has held firm, and his superiors in central government have evidently told him that the time has come to face the renegades himself. He does not appear to be relishing the prospect. He creeps half-heartedly up the hill and is immediately surrounded by an angry crowd. He hurriedly calls Plazarte over to him, and refuses to speak until Judith Hidalgo is also present, presumably in the hope that she will protect him from the mob. People fire questions and accusations at him, but he ignores them, picking distractedly at his nose and shifting from foot to foot like a nervous toddler waiting for his mom.

Judith arrives, and the governor reluctantly delivers his speech in a small, timorous voice. The *paro* must be abandoned immediately, he says, and everyone must return to work tomorrow, because the local economy is suffering, and the state is losing oil revenues. "The idea," he explains, dutifully reciting lines that he knows will be met with derision, "is to resume normal activities and, parallel to that, to begin negotiations because in this way…" Before he can finish, his voice is lost in the tumult of the crowd, and Olger Naichap steps forward to confront him. "I don't understand the situation," Olger begins, with exaggerated ingenuousness. "Why are you annoyed with us? Why do you feel obliged to demand that we allow CGA to resume its operations?" The governor repeats his lines. Olger waits politely for him to finish, before posing another question. "Now, why are you going around stirring up trouble?" he asks, in reference to the countermovement. Malla begins to respond again, but this time Olger immediately cuts him off: "The Ecuadorian state says that [national oil] production is being damaged. In the same way, when the company doesn't pay us a fair salary, it is damaging our children's future."

This comparison draws shouts of agreement from the crowd, and Olger begins to wind himself into full warrior mode. "Pardon me, but this is my style!" he explains to Malla, as if apologizing in advance for the hellfire that he is about to unleash upon him. "This is the voice of the people! My father made me a man! And here I am!" he roars, flexing his muscles and drawing closer to the craven governor. "We are happy to stay here day and night, and we will not back down until this situation is resolved!" He turns to the crowd, and points at the miserable spectacle of Colon Malla, who stands flat-footed, with one arm folded under the other, resting his flabby face dejectedly on a chubby hand. "Who elected the governor?" Olger asks rhetorically. The obvious answer is "No one" – the governor is appointed directly by the Ecuadorian president – and this shameful word is flung in Malla's face with immense gusto by the crowd. "No-one elected the governor," Olger confirms. "If the governor doesn't do what the president wants, he will be fired. He's just defending his job, *compañeros*. Those who are with the people, let them stand with the people," he concludes, fixing the governor with a steady gaze, "And those who are not with the people? Well, let them go with CGA! *Hasta la victoria siempre compañeros!*"

The governor shrugs. "Well, see you on Tuesday then," he mumbles morosely, and begins shuffling away. But his ritual humiliation is not yet complete. His path is cut off by Bolívar Naichap and Marco Kapáku – the presidents of their respective communities, who launch into a particularly aggressive version of the *Saludo Shuar*, which is performed not only when greeting allies, but also when confronting the authorities. The cops have already retreated, and Malla is stranded on his own in the middle of the street. The *Shuar* who are gathered around him all seem to know what is about to happen, although they can't quite believe it. They are smiling in astonished anticipation, and one of the women is already laughing behind her hand. But poor old Colon Malla isn't in on the joke. He's trying to hold it together, but his eyes are darting, and his smile is forced. Suddenly the two leaders rush toward him, spears poised above their heads, screaming the seemingly blood-curdling battle cry that is in fact a call to unity. Malla tries to spread his smile across his face, but it won't stretch that far and gets stuck halfway. Finally, they drive their spears past him, missing him by a good distance, and the entire crowd erupts in laughter, including the relieved giggle of the governor himself.

*****

This has been a good day for the *paro*. The countermovement has been defeated, the man from the Oil Ministry has been ridiculed, the governor has been reprimanded, and the struggle has grown in strength and unity. In the evening, Judith Hidalgo invites me to join her and a small group of *Shuar* women on the warm asphalt of the Savage Road. "Come and sit with us on our sofa!" she says cheerfully. I tell them that I enjoyed the symbolic spearing of the governor. "That was nothing," Judith replies, "We've reduced politicians to tears before now!" The other women fall around laughing as they imagine what was going through Colon Malla's head as the spears whistled past his ears. He must have been praying to God, they say, and promising that if he survives, he will mend his ways and stop defending the company.

It was a brilliant piece of carnivalesque political theater, in which the unfortunate governor was cast in the role of the state being forced to bow to the sovereignty of the people. But to what extent do such performances really challenge dominant power relations? And to what extent do they provide the comic relief of a symbolic inversion of those relations, which ultimately contributes to the reproduction of the status quo? Perhaps this is the true function of a figure like the governor – a clown-like representation of the state, who submits himself to acts of popular debasement in order to provide the people with an illusory sense of power. Gonzalo Plazarte is staying late at the *paro* this evening – still playing his ambiguous role of mediator and confidante – and when I speak with him, he concurs with this assessment of the day's events. From his point of view, the dramatic twists and turns are all part of the strategy of the company, which is "to keep the people going round and round in circles."

Later that evening, I am at last allowed into the inner sanctum of the *paro* – the hidden headquarters in the gorge beneath the roadside, where the leaders of the *comité* organize and strategize and avoid arrest. I have been trying to get in here to interview the leaders since the second day of the uprising, but have always been refused. But I had my second article on the *paro* published online today, and I stood with the *Shuar* women throughout the confrontation in the coliseum, and this seems to have been enough to finally gain the trust of the leadership. I am led into a makeshift single-room hut of planks and plastic sheeting, where a group of men are seated around a wooden table, in darkness broken only by the light of mobile phones. I explain that I would like to interview them for my next press release, to make sure I am communicating the message that they want to be heard. The two main leaders – Darío and Méndez – are not here. Instead, I am addressed by the next in command, while the others listen in silence:

> You have been a witness, a supporter [of our struggle, while] the press of our own country chooses to ignore us. We have no problem with you reporting

> everything you have seen without missing out a single detail … As you will have noticed, the *paro* is becoming increasingly radical, and more people and communities are joining. Up until this moment, the *paro* has been peaceful. Transport has been flowing normally … But off the record I can tell you that if there is no solution on Tuesday, all forty communities of the parish will unite with the workers and the Indigenous communities in this struggle against racist abuse and labor exploitation, and we will shut down oil production throughout Block 61.

*****

In the final three days before the negotiations, the *paro* is a hive of activity. The negotiations will be held in the coliseum, and it must be rammed to the rafters. A spear factory has been set up in a tent at the edge of the *paro* to provide weapons for everyone on the day, and hundreds of invitations have been printed out on little strips of paper, for distribution to passing traffic. The invitations are a statement of proletarian unity, signed by representatives of local Indigenous organizations and the *comité*, and describing the negotiations as a "mobilization of communities and parishes in the battle … for a transformation of working conditions in Block 61." Whenever a bus approaches, Bolívar Naichap blocks its path, and Tigrillo clambers aboard to hand them out. Along with several of his mestizo comrades, Tigrillo is embracing the collective "Indigenous" identity of the *paro* with increasing gusto. Each time he boards a bus, he does so not in the denim overalls of an oil worker, but stripped to the waist and adorned with *Shuar* jewelry and *achiote* designs.

Meanwhile, Edison Kapáku has been reading up on labor rights, the right to resistance, and the law banning *tercerización*, and is reporting his discoveries to the rest of the *paro*, in order to prepare them for the negotiations. And Pablo Gallegos – the Carmelite priest who confronted the pedantic bureaucrat on the first day of the *paro* – drops by to give an impromptu lecture. It is a skilled piece of popular pedagogy, delivered to workers without much formal education and with little prior experience of labor militancy, and blending earthy humor and personal recollections with snatches of Marxist theory:

> You must maintain the *paro*. You are doing well so far … But you have taken this decision and it is vital that you stick with it. The head is out, and now the rest of the body has to come out as well. The whole baby! (He gets a good laugh for this) … I remember the first great conflict of this kind [in the Ecuadorian Amazon]. It was against … a company that had over a thousand workers [just like CGA] … The *paro* lasted a long time. They demanded better hours, better food, better treatment … It was the same thing – the improvement of working conditions. And here we will always be in conflict, because capital and labor, capitalists and workers, have different interests, don't they? The capitalist wants to make as much money as possible, and the worker wants to improve life for their family. You know that you have the full support of the mission in everything you need. We are here to contribute [to your struggle].

This is liberation theology without the theology! More importantly, it is Marxism without obscurantism, and everyone immediately grasps the message and recognizes it as resonating with their own lived experience. Gallegos tells a few more stories, cracks a few more jokes, and catches the next bus out of town, promising to return for the negotiations on Tuesday.

But on Monday morning the mood darkens again. Representatives of the *comité* have been going through the smartphone of Esteban García, the operations manager of CGA, which was confiscated during his kidnapping. They have discovered the communications of a WhatsApp group formed by García and other members of the CGA management. The messages are revelatory in several ways. They include the sharing of racist memes about Indigenous peoples, and they demonstrate that CGA has been paying for the presence of the army at the *paro*, ostensibly to cover the cost of the soldiers' meals. Of more immediate concern, however, is an apparent murder plot targeting two key members of the *paro*.

The plot dates from August 24, shortly after the *comuna* of Kapáku had first shut down the oil platform on their territory, in conjunction with the launch of the initial sit-down strike. Screenshots from the messages of the WhatsApp group show images of a blockaded bridge at the entrance to the platform, which were posted by one of the managers, along with a message explaining that operations have been suspended, which blames Marco Kapáku for the disruption. A second manager responds: "We need to kill that guy. He's the biggest idiot of them all" (*lo mas pelotudo que hay*). First manager: "It's unbelievable. And the *negro* of the *comité*" (referring to Darío, who is Black.) Second manager: "He's even worse. Another who needs to be killed." First manager: "We need to get them together on the bridge and destroy them (*tumbarlos*)."

This could be idle talk. But the murder of activists disrupting the operation of extractive industries is a regular occurrence throughout South America, and everyone at the *paro* is taking it very seriously. An official complaint has been lodged with the public prosecutor in Coca, although no one expects it to be acted upon. Faced with this threat to his life, Marco Kapáku addresses the somber crowd:

> This must not distract us from our struggle *compañeros*. It is of no importance to me if someone wants to damage my person. I was not born to live like a stone (*Yo no nací para hacerme piedra.*) It's better to die fighting … And when we win, we will have a fiesta in my community *compañeros*! We have [an oil] platform that has been set up perfectly for a fiesta! It has floodlights! We can put them all on and shine them on everyone, so that everyone can dance all night *compañeros*! We have no lack of music – the parish council has given us their sound system. So, we are going to have a big party *compañeros*! And why? Because by then we will have destroyed *them*! Now we have them scared, these CGA. Now it's nine days that they are not operating, and that hurts CGA, because CGA is losing [money]. We will hold firm! This is how we fight *compañeros*! *Viva el paro!*

It is a courageous speech, and long before its conclusion, the dread that had seized the crowd has been replaced once more with defiant jubilation. But everyone knows the stakes have just been raised again. Tomorrow's negotiations will not only be with a racist, exploitative company, but with a company whose managers have discussed murdering the men who face them across the table.

*****

At around midday, I return to my hotel room to notify my contacts in Quito about this new development. Half an hour later, a knock comes on my door. It's a member of staff from the hotel. "The police are looking for you," he whispers, "what should I tell them?" I freeze. I had been fearing something like this ever since the confrontation in the coliseum. But I had somehow neglected to give any thought to what I would do if it actually happened. "Tell them I'm not here," I suggest, in the absence of any better ideas. "I already told them that," he replies, "They say they know you're here." I try to think fast. I need to buy enough time to get a message to the *paro*. "Tell them …" My voice trails off, and we both wait for my panicked brain to function. "Tell them I'm in the shower, and I'll be down in a couple of minutes." He nods and hurries away. I scrabble through my papers in search of my phone, trying not to think about the story a human rights activist told me a few days ago in Coca, about a journalist who was covering a *paro* back in 2006. He had been seized by the cops and disappeared, before showing up half-dead in a ditch two days later.[6] I find my phone and call Edison Kapáku. By a miracle he picks up and I hastily explain the situation. He listens in silence. "Which hotel are you in?" he asks. "Hotel Guerrero" I reply. "We're on our way" he says and hangs up.

I hear a motorbike approaching at speed from down the hill. It must be them. I badly need it to be them. I close the door behind me and descend the stairs. Two police officers are waiting for me in the lobby, accompanied by a third man in plain clothes. Before any of us has time to speak, the motorbike screeches to a halt outside. It is driven by a guy from the *paro*, and Tigrillo is on the back. Good old Tigrillo – scrawny-ribbed, missing-toothed, and armed with a very nasty looking spear.

"Thank fuck for that!" I think. "I understand you're looking for me?" I say. The cops say nothing. But the man in plain clothes wants to see my passport – he is clearly running the operation. I go upstairs to fetch it, and by the time I get back at least 50 more people from the *paro* have arrived, led by Bolívar Naichap. The hotel lobby is open-sided, and the whole entrance is now filled with renegades, many with their faces masked and all armed with spears. I hand my passport over to the man in plain clothes. But before he can open it, Bolívar demands to see his police ID. It hadn't occurred to me to question whether the guy was actually a cop, but now he is refusing to produce the document. The demands grow more widespread and insistent, and I notice that his hands are trembling. Eventually, he shows them his national ID card – the same one carried by all Ecuadorians, and nothing to do with the police force. Now people are screaming that he is a *sapo* – a toad, a spy, an infiltrator. A spear is thrust out of the crowd and comes to a stop about an inch from his forehead. "Give him back his passport," says Bolívar Naichap. The fake cop does so without a second glance – his gaze is firmly fixed on the spear that now rests between his eyes. I run to my room, grab my laptop and any other potentially incriminating material that immediately comes to mind, and rush back downstairs and onto the street, where the crowd forms a protective circle around me. By now the rest of the road is filled with people not involved in the *paro*, some of whom I recognize from the phony countermovement. Looking back at the entrance to the lobby, I can see the fake cop being interrogated by Bolívar and several others, while the two police officers look on in impotent passivity. Bolívar makes the fake cop remove his baseball cap, and photographs are taken of his fully revealed face. Then we all walk back down the hill together, while the rest of the town watches us in silence.

Back at the blockade, I thank Edison and everyone else for coming to my rescue, and for the first and only time I lead a shout of "*Viva el paro!*" Tigrillo and the other guy who were first to arrive are having a great time doing impressions of the fear on my white face when they first got there. "He was *pálido!*" says Tigrillo with his toothless laugh. "Even more pallid than usual!" says the other. There are competing theories about the identity of the fake cop. Some say he's just a common toad, who had been seen lurking around the *paro* before. But others think he could be a *sicario* – a hitman, and that if they hadn't shown up when they did, I would have been smuggled out of town and never seen again. Either way, everyone is adamant that this is the work of the company, and that it further demonstrates the extent to which the police are acting on its instructions.

Pablo Gallegos calls me a few minutes later. He has heard about what has happened. He tells me not to go anywhere alone from now on, and to sleep at the *paro* instead of returning to my hotel. But I need to go back there briefly to get the rest of my things, and to upload the last of my information. I explain the situation to Edison, and he organizes a group of militants to accompany me, led by Linda Kapáku and Juan Santiak – a veteran of the 1998 war with Peru.

This is my first night of "dawning" with the *paro*. The evening meal arrives around half past eight, and once it's finished most people head for home. Only 40 or so remain – the most die-hard foot-soldiers of the uprising, rather than the leaders: people like Linda, Santiak, Tigrillo, and Pedro – the pug-faced dude who threw out the *sapos* on the third day. Most of them stretch out on wooden planks and rows of oil pipes and try to get some sleep, while a few small groups keep watch on the road. As the night draws on, the traffic decreases, and soon the only vehicles are cop cars patrolling the perimeters of the *Obrador Central*. Each time they pass I am ushered out of sight, down a slope that leads toward the remains of an abandoned hut that had been built beneath the pipelines. After this has happened a few times, Linda suggests that it would be best for me to sleep down here. She finds a piece of cardboard for a mattress and a cardigan for a blanket. I spread the cardboard on the concrete patio and lie down, feeling the last of the adrenaline draining from my veins. Santiak settles down to sleep nearby, his spear held to his chest. The starlight flickers between the pipelines, the cicadas intensify their screeching chorus, and drunken calls of "*viva el paro*" drift down from the Savage Road.

*****

Linda wakes me at dawn, with a cup of coffee and a chunk of bread. The entire Kapáku clan is here by 7am, followed by a steady stream of Indigenous and mestizo groups from across Block 61 and beyond. The printed invitation has clearly been effective, and the news of the murder plot has also spread quickly and has galvanized support for the struggle. By 8am, there are already at least four hundred people at the blockade. Journalists and television crews also begin to arrive, including Teleamazonas, the leading national news channel – the first time any major news organization has covered the *paro*. Pablo Gallegos is here, and so is Enrique Morales – the strategic mastermind of the ABP, who led the triumphant negotiations that concluded the legendary *paro* of 2005.

Everyone is waiting for the negotiations, which are scheduled to begin at 10am. In the meantime, the *Shuar* communities assemble at the top of the hill and march down through the crowd, chanting a militant refrain and thrusting their spears into the air. Many of the men are painted jet black from head to toe – a mixture of charcoal and water that is worn to represent the drenching of the region in the dark social relations and destructive material flows of the oil industry.[7] They are led by Marco Kapáku – the *Shuar* leader who the company managers were planning to have killed. At the bottom of the hill, they break into the rapid and intricate dance of the *jempe* – the hummingbird that risked its life to steal the secret of fire, which it bore to the *Shuar* on its own burning wings.[8] This dance of valiant insurrection is entwined with a *Kichwa* ritual performed in confrontations with the oil industry, in which a solitary male figure adopts the sinister persona of petroleum itself. His body stained with charcoal, and with the charred skulls of two collared peccaries strapped to his head and neck, the oil man weaves diabolically between the spiraling fire dancers.

The impromptu fusion of these powerful *Shuar* and *Kichwa* rituals conveys the tense and menacing atmosphere that has descended on the *paro*, in contrast to the joyful dances of previous days. Then Olger Naichap seizes the mic and signals for the music to cease. His scowling face is charcoal black. The rest of the dancers line up at his back bearing their spears, as the television cameras and microphones jostle for space around him:

> I will begin by greeting my *pueblo*: *Viva el pueblo Shuar! Viva el pueblo Huaorani!* Long live the *Kichwa* nation! Long live the workers! … We are not going to allow this company to keep mistreating our *pueblo* … All those messages on social media between the big shots (*los duros*) … saying "We have to kill that guy" – let them do it if they can! We, as *pueblos* and nations, do not fear death. That is why, as *pueblos* and as workers, we [dare to] demand our rights. I want the media to transmit this message to the authorities of the nation: If this company doesn't have the capacity to sort

> out this situation, then they had better get their things and get out! Because in Dayuma there are brave and angry people (*gente brava*)! ... We do not fear them! We will not be humiliated by them! They come here to make their money and mistreat us. Where is the law? Where are our authorities? Perhaps they have been paid off, and that is why they won't defend the rights of their own *pueblo*. But Dayuma is a *pueblo* that deserves respect ... Here the *pueblo Shuar*, the *pueblo colono* and the four parishes will remain united ... And if the company and the authorities don't solve this situation today, then we won't just paralyze CGA. We will paralyze the whole of Schlumberger and Petroamazonas *compañeros*!

Olger has worked himself into a towering rage over the course of his speech, and each line has been greeted by a roar from the crowd still louder than the last. Once again, the central message is an assertion of universal humanity – Indigenous and *colono*, *pueblo* and worker, against the Machiavellian machinations of capital and the corrupt servility of the state. By the end, as he announces the collective intention to shut down oil production throughout the Savage Road, everyone is shaking their spears above their heads, Edison Kapáku is hollering "That's it! That's it!" at the top of his voice, and Linda Kapáku faints and has to be carried out of the crowd.

Other leaders now take their turns to speak to the media. Darío Rodríguez, general secretary of the *comité* and the second target of the murder plot, reads out the incriminating WhatsApp messages. Jhon Rosero presents a detailed analysis of the Schlumberger contract for Block 61, and insists that the central focus on the negotiations must be the end of *tercerización* and the payment of *utilidades* to the workers. And Marco Kapáku reaffirms the universality of the *paro*, and its simultaneous embodiment and transcendence of racial and ethnic differences: "We are different nationalities. We are *Shuar*, *Kichwa*, *Huaorani*, *colono*, from different communities. We have united to defend the rights that every worker deserves."

By the time they have finished it is past 10am, and the majority of the *paro* departs for the coliseum. A small contingent must remain, however, to guard against any attempt by the army to seize control of the *Obrador Central* during the negotiations. Edison Kapáku asks me to stay with them, to bear witness to any such event. Before long, however, it becomes clear to those of us at the blockade that something is amiss. The morning is almost over and there is still no sign of the ministerial delegation, or the management of CGA. Finally, at around 1pm, a motorcade of police cars and SUVs with blacked-out windows glides past us into Dayuma. But it turns out to only contain the governor, who explains to the packed coliseum that the managers of CGA fear for their safety in Dayuma, and that they are again demanding that the negotiations be held behind closed doors in Coca. Their fear is understandable, given the discovery of their murderous plotting. But this is a violation of one of the fundamental conditions of the negotiations, and it is immediately rejected. Before long, the governor's convoy rolls past us again, on its way back to Coca, with the situation unresolved.

The leaders of the *paro* stay in the coliseum, while we remain at the blockade awaiting further news. The afternoon is hot and stagnant, and there is a sense of claustrophobic desperation in the air. A guy from my hotel stops by on a motorbike to tell me that the police have just been there again, trying to get my passport details. I'm going to have to get out of here very soon, no matter what happens with these non-existent negotiations. Then Tilapia shows up on the back of a truck, and motions for me to jump in. The negotiations are about to begin after all, he says, and the *comité* wants me to report on them. But it turns out to be yet another false hope. The ministers and oil executives were apparently headed in this direction. But instead of coming here they entered Auca Central, the heavily fortified oil station of Petroamazonas, which processes all the oil produced in Block 61. The coliseum is still packed. But on hearing this news people give up and begin to drift away.

Moments later, there is a rush of activity at the entrance, and exultant cries of "*La prefecta! La prefecta!*" Pursued by an entourage of *comité* leaders and parish council presidents, Guadalupe Llori, the legendary prefect of Orellana, sweeps into the auditorium with regal authority. All hail the heroine of the historic *paros*! All hail the rebel prefect imprisoned by Correa! Everyone who has just left the building is running back inside, and everyone else is hushed and focused on the empty table in the center, where the delegation was supposed to be, and where Llori now takes hold of the microphone. Her voice is deep and resonant. She shakes her fist as she speaks, and her big hoop earrings and thick gold necklaces shimmer in the afternoon sunlight bursting through the open sides of the coliseum:

> I spent fifteen years fighting on the streets! In the time of the *paros* I didn't miss a single one! They called me a "stone thrower" (*tira piedras* – one of Correa's favored insults with which to ridicule and criminalize dissent). Maybe so, but the stone is the only weapon of the poor! … But this is what I want to tell you *compañeros*: We must learn to negotiate! And we will not get everything we ask for. Remember, I have been in very tough fights in the past (*vengo de peleas bien duras*) … So *compañeros*, they are telling us that they will not come here to negotiate? OK then! In that case, we will go to Auca Central! … Everyone! Every single one of us!

Her message is simple: CGA is reneging on their agreement on the location of the negotiations and is insisting on holding them in Coca. But that need not leave us in the hopeless position of either capitulating to their demands or abandoning the negotiations completely. Instead, we need to alter our own approach – ambush them in Auca Central and force them to negotiate there, with everyone present. The effect on the crowd is instant and dramatic. Before she has finished, her voice is drowned out by a unanimous roar of agreement and the rumble of hundreds of people running to the doors. These few words from this famous renegade leader have flipped the entire dynamic on its head. A suffocating sense of impossibility has been suddenly transformed into an explosion of insurrectional energy. All around me people are laughing, embracing, and shouting "*Viva el paro!*" as we surge out of the coliseum, onto motorbikes and flatbeds, and into pickups and dump trucks. I scramble onto the back of one of the pickups, and soon we are rushing past the blockade, past a line of cop cars, and out onto the open road. The atmosphere is simultaneously ecstatic and confrontational, raging and liberating. Our pickup heads the convoy, followed by a legion of motorbikes all blaring their horns – a motley biker gang racing through the oil wastelands.

*****

We swing into the forecourt of Auca Central about 15 minutes later, just in time to meet a column of heavily armed soldiers marching swiftly across the station to cut us off at the front gates. The installations are vast, including offices, apartments, a restaurant, a conference center, an airstrip, and a labyrinth of pipes and cylinders, with gas flares burning low between the trees and belching fitful fireballs into the evening sky. Soon there are at least a thousand people here, amassed on an open hillside that stretches up from the road opposite the oil station. Everyone, it seems, is now supporting the struggle. The woman who cleans the rooms in my hotel is here, as are several people from the so-called countermovement, and even the local businessman who accosted me in the restaurant and told me that he was opposed to the *paro*. Gonzalo Plazarte appears to have finally thrown his weight fully behind the workers and is now bare-chested and carrying a spear. The only people conspicuous by their absence are the fake cop and the disgraced Wilmer Armas.

Word soon arrives that CGA have agreed to negotiate. But they are still insisting that the negotiation take place with a vetted delegation behind closed doors. The decision is swiftly taken to accept these terms on two conditions: First, that everyone else will remain outside the gates. And second, that Chimbo and Charango – the loathsome organizers of the countermarch – are immediately expelled from the premises, where they have been discovered to be lurking. Minutes later, they emerge from the gates under police guard, and scurry to the safety of a cop car amidst a torrent of delighted abuse. Then Darío draws up a list of delegates, including the leading members of the *comité*, and representatives of the Indigenous communities and the unemployed. Judith Hidalgo will also take part, along with Enrique Morales, Pablo Gallegos, and Guadalupe Llori.

The delegation is admitted one by one, without their spears or mobile phones. Soon afterwards, a truck arrives with an enormous tank of drinking water, followed by a pickup filled with sweetbread and vats of coffee. Night falls and the hours drag by without news. The mood on the street is febrile, veering back and forth between fury and elation. One moment everyone is dancing to an acapella singsong, the next they are screaming at the soldiers for their abject treachery; one moment everyone is chanting that "the people united will never be defeated," the next they are muttering about dirty deals done behind closed doors; one moment everyone is happily eating sweetbread, the next they are furiously rushing at the gates, demanding to know what is going on inside.

A full moon rises over ragged clouds. The gas flare billows like a midnight sun behind the trees. Bright stars. Distant lightning. I am physically, mentally, and emotionally exhausted. And this is only my second night of "dawning." I cannot imagine the fatigue of those who have been doing this since the start. And meanwhile their adversaries slept sweetly, biding their time in their distant mansions and luxury hotels. I lie back on the road that runs up the hillside opposite the oil station. The soldiers are still lined up behind the gates, silhouetted by the floodlights. I sink into the dark warmth of the sun-filled road.

At 3am, a shout goes up for us to return to the gates. Jhon Rosero announces that the negotiations have concluded, and an agreement has been signed. Soon afterwards, the delegation emerges, led by Guadalupe Llori, who reads out the details of the accord. The main outcome is that CGA have agreed to submit to a full review of their activities by the Labor Ministry, to establish whether they are complying with Ecuadorian law, and whether this is indeed a case of *tercerización*. The review will last 20 working days, with the verdict to be pronounced on October 5 – precisely one month from now. In the meantime, the *paro* has been suspended and everyone will return to work, beginning tomorrow. No further action will be taken against the *comité* or any of the participants in the *paro*. And all workers will be fully paid for all the days of work missed during the blockade.

This last point raises a particularly enthusiastic cheer. But everyone knows that the battle against this monster is very far from over. Everything now rests on the outcome of the Labor Ministry's review. And given the general tendency for the Ecuadorian state to cravenly serve the interests of the oil companies, and the specific issue of the billion-or-so dollars that the current cash-strapped administration owes to Schlumberger in revenues for the oil extracted from Block 61, it is hard to imagine that the Ministry will conclude in favor of the workers. Have we walked into a trap?

Footage included in a local news report filmed inside Auca Central illustrates the power dynamics that come into play once a small delegation of renegades is locked into negotiations behind closed doors on enemy territory. In contrast to the anarchic space of the blockade, the conference hall is infused with the bland anonymity of bureaucratic authority. The ministers and oil executives are sitting together on a raised stage, looking down on the delegation from the *paro*, who languish in the rows of seats that fill the auditorium, like naughty students being told off at school assembly. Olger Naichap is still stripped to the waist and covered in charcoal, and Marco Kapáku still wears a toucan feather headdress reserved for the most courageous *Shuar* leaders in times of battle. But what were powerful symbols of rebellion on the street look like bad fancy dress in the midst of this anodyne Western modernity, beneath the disdainful gaze of suited white men.

The end of Llori's speech outside the gates is met with cries of "*Gracias!*" and "*Viva la prefecta!*" But to what extent did her intervention in the coliseum really work in favor of the *paro*, and to what extent did it play into the hands of state and capital, by leading the rebels into this apparent cul-de-sac? People are embracing and congratulating each other. But the atmosphere is subdued. There is no great celebration, no "caravan of struggle." Everyone is shattered, and soon the workers must return to the grind, while the jobless must remain in their precarity. Despite their central role in the struggle, the unemployed have gained nothing from tonight's accord, and the jobs promised to them have not materialized. Santiak mutters something to this effect as we begin to disperse. He has had my back all day, while Linda has been keeping a close eye on the cops. Now they smuggle me into the back of a covered flatbed truck and tell me to lie down so that I won't be seen as we leave. The first roosters have begun to crow as we pass the abandoned blockade on our return to Dayuma. We sneak into a hastily opened restaurant and knock back the beers as fast as we can. But daylight is coming, and I no longer have the *paro* to protect me from the police. The first bus to Coca comes by just before dawn. I down my drink, say my goodbyes, and jump on board.

6 Grand Inferno

Sunday morning at the Hotel Guerrero. Nursing a hangover in the stagnant heat. Grimy vultures circling over sullen jungle. Evangelical hymns mingling with the screams of a circular saw. It's August 2018, and I'm back in Dayuma, almost a year after the *paro*. For eleven months, I served my time in a northern European university, distractedly fulfilling my academic duties, and counting the days before returning to the Amazon. When I finally got back here, I spent the first few days in Coca, trying to find out what had happened in my absence, and handing out copies of an article on the *paro* that I had published in the Ecuadorian press shortly after my hasty departure from the region. The oil price had improved somewhat in the interim, and the previously desolate town center was starting to gleam once again with the grubby opulence of peripheral petrodollars.

The first person I looked up was Enrique Morales – the ABP veteran who had advised the *comité* in their negotiations with the government and CGA. He brought me up to date with the situation and put me in touch with Darío Rodríguez and Manuel Méndez, the principal representatives of the *comité*. They invited me out to Méndez's place, where they were having a reunion. His house was on the Savage Road, about halfway between Coca and Dayuma. We sat outside around plastic tables, chewing on sugar cane from his *finca*, and rapidly emptying many crates of beer, while discussing the *paro* and its aftermath. My hangover has erased most of our conversation. But I remember one phrase that Méndez shouted at the night sky, amidst the raucous cheers of his comrades: "*Pueblo chico, infierno grande!*"

The phrase translates as "Small town, big hell!" It's a common expression across Latin America, where it refers to the rumor and innuendo that plague the everyday life of small towns throughout the region. But here they take it literally, as Méndez explained: "Dayuma is a small town, but we raise a lot of hell!" And yes, they had raised all kinds of hell while I had been away.

*****

The agreement signed by CGA, the government, and the delegation of the *paro* in the early hours of September 6, 2017, had committed the Labor Ministry to conduct a full investigation of the company's operations, and to report its findings

DOI: 10.4324/9781003345879-6

on October 5 – one month later. In return, the *paro* had been suspended, and everyone had returned to work the following day. But there was little indication that the promised investigation was actually taking place, and as the deadline approached, the *comité* began preparing for a resumption of hostilities. On the morning of October 5, the leaders of the *comité* arrived at the *Obrador Central*, headed by Darío and Méndez, and announced the launch of another *paro*, which would continue until the Labor Ministry delivered its report. Fearing a repeat of the previous uprising, which had begun with the storming of the camp and the kidnapping of its operations manager, CGA responded by immediately expelling all workers from the installations and locking the gates.

Later that morning, Colon Malla, the universally detested governor of Orellana, arrived at the *Obrador Central*. Standing alongside Colonel Wilson Tualombo, and backed by soldiers and police, he informed the striking workers that the report was not complete and announced a new date for its delivery: October 20 – over two weeks away. In the meantime, they were to return to work immediately. According to a private security report produced for CGA, "After the speech by the governor, the situation became increasingly tense." Indigenous communities began arriving to support the strikers, at which point the management "decided to demobilize all remaining personnel, with the aim of avoiding incidents that would compromise their personal security." In the genteel language of the report, "the demonstrators behaved in an aggressive and hostile manner toward the functionaries, who were obliged to remove themselves under police protection ... [while] threats to seize and sack the installations became increasingly effusive."[1]

The standoff was maintained over the course of the following days, with police and soldiers stationed inside the *Obrador*, and the blockade continuing outside. This situation was developing in parallel with increasing tensions between Schlumberger and the Ecuadorian government, which now owed Schlumberger $1.1 billion of unpaid revenues for the oil extracted from Block 61. On October 11, one week into the second *paro*, Schlumberger's stock price slumped, following a credit downgrade from the investment bank BMO Capital Markets, which identified the scale of the Ecuadorian debt to the company as the primary cause for concern.[2] Two days later, the *paro* upped the ante by preventing the circulation of all vehicles related to the oil industry. Blockades multiplied along the Savage Road, to cut off access roads to oil wells located between Coca and Dayuma.

Now it was not only the construction of new oil infrastructure that was being blocked, but also the servicing of existing wells, without which the production of Block 61 – and that of other oil blocks along the Savage Road – would rapidly diminish. The tactic had its intended effect. Schlumberger and the government promptly agreed to fresh negotiations, to be held in Auca Central on October 19, at which the Labor Ministry would finally deliver its long-awaited report. That was five days away. In the meantime, the blockades remained in place. The wells began running out of diesel and other supplies, and the flow of oil started to decline.

In contrast to the first *paro*, which had been largely ignored by the rest of the country, the increased radicalism of the second *paro* was drawing the attention of national political movements and organizations. As the date of the negotiations approached, the presidents of the principal national and regional Indigenous organizations – the Confederation of National Indigenous Organizations of Ecuador (CONAIE) and the Confederation of Amazonian Indigenous Nations of Ecuador (CONFENIAE) – both announced their participation. The leaders of the Amazonian *Shuar*, *Kichwa*, and *Huaorani* organizations would also be present. Their involvement raised the profile of the *paro* and added to the growing pressure on the government to resolve the situation. But it also generated tensions within the movement, as each organization sought to defend its constituency, and to frame the *paro* in its own terms. These problems first emerged in discussions over the agenda of the negotiations. Each of the Indigenous organizations wanted to include its own demands, and the parish councils and provincial government also began to press for the inclusion of demands unrelated to the original uprising. As tensions grew, rumors began to circulate that individual groups were conspiring with the governor and the company to advance their own interests at the expense of the others, and that certain leaders had taken payoffs to undermine the *paro*.

Negotiations began as planned on the morning of October 19. As had been the case in previous rounds, the delegation of the *paro* included the leaders of the *comité* and representatives of the *Shuar comunas* that had been involved from the start. But this time the prefect of Orellana, Guadalupe Llori, and the president of the parish council of Dayuma, Judith Hidalgo, were both excluded from the proceedings. And when Jaime Vargas, the president of CONAIE, arrived at the gates of Auca Central to join the negotiations, he was denied entry by Darío Rodríguez, who accused CONAIE of trying to hijack the struggle with their own agenda. It was a bold move on the part of the Afro-descendant leader, which had the support of the Indigenous members of the delegation. But a snub of such monumental proportions was bound to have consequences. After all, Darío was just a young provincial renegade, while Jaime Vargas was the head of an internationally respected Indigenous movement, and arguably the most prominent radical political leader in the country. Together with the president of CONFENIAE, who had also been denied entry by Darío, Vargas then met with a large contingent of *Shuar*, *Kichwa*, and *Huaorani* from the parish of Inés Arango, who were marching to Auca Central to demand jobs with CGA. This was the first time the *Huaorani* had shown up at the *paro* in force, and they were about to live up to their reputation for drastically upping the stakes of any struggle in which they become involved.

Vargas informed the marchers that CONAIE had been barred from the negotiations, which he framed as an act of aggression against Indigenous peoples, before warning them that they would also be refused entry. On this basis, the march turned around and headed for Dayuma, where Judith Hidalgo was holding a meeting of her parishioners in the coliseum, following her own exclusion from the negotiations. Amidst all the rumors of double dealings and personal agendas that had been circulating over the previous days, Judith's name had been the one most frequently repeated. She was accused of scheming with the company and the governor to ensure that all available jobs went to her parishioners, instead of those from the other three parishes of the Savage Road. And right now, she was meeting with those very same parishioners in Dayuma, behind the backs of the Indigenous communities of Inés Arango, while her co-conspirators were doing her dirty work for her behind closed doors in Auca Central. It was all stitch up, and Judith Hidalgo was to blame!

Footage broadcast on national television captures the arrival of the Indigenous march in Dayuma. Hundreds of spear-wielding *Shuar*, *Kichwa*, and *Huaorani* women and men are rushing into the cavernous coliseum. They are heading for the stage at the far end of the room, while the local parishioners scramble out of their way, and the speakers try to escape. The clip then cuts to a closeup of Judith Hidalgo. "I will not negotiate with Inés Arango!" she stammers breathlessly. She is pinned into the corner of the stage, with her entourage crushed tightly around her.[3] According to several witnesses, the *Huaorani* were determined to lynch her, and she narrowly escaped with her life. In the words of one *Kichwa* parish councilor:

> The *Huao* arrived, wanting to kill *la señora presidenta*. Due to a misunderstanding, they were saying that *la señora presidenta* had received money from the company. So they arrived with spears. But as we were standing beside her, we grabbed *la presidenta* and got her out of there. Otherwise she would be dead. They broke the microphone, broke the chairs, broke the tables.[4]

The coliseum of Dayuma had been seized and occupied by the Indigenous communities of the neighboring parish. Mobile phone footage shows Jaime Vargas taking the stage to address the crowd:

> We are here to support your struggle! Because CONAIE *is* you! And we have always said that we will defend the rights of the *pueblos* and [First] Nations of Ecuador. *Compañeros*, we were invited to a meeting [in Auca Central]. But it turned out that they had shut themselves inside, in a little room, and they left us [outside], while they took the decisions.

His voice is drowned out by shouts of indignation. The camera pans the coliseum, which is absolutely rammed, everyone with spears aloft. The president of CONFENIAE then speaks, followed by leaders of the regional *Huaorani*, *Kichwa*, and *Shuar* associations. None of the speakers has been involved in the struggle until this point, and each has a similar message of ethnic division. "I have a question for our *colono* brothers", the representative of the *Shuar* begins, "How many *indígenas* are working [for the company]?" He is waving his finger furiously in the faces of his imaginary *colono* enemies. "Not even ten percent. Who is working? Our *colono* brothers! Forgive me, but with the greatest respect, they are one hundred percent *compañeros!*"[5]

The speeches conclude with the unanimous decision to return to Inés Arango and launch a *paro* of their own, regardless of the outcome of the negotiations in Auca Central. In retrospect, almost everyone I spoke to identified this event as the key moment of division, the point at which the spontaneous eruption of universal humanity that had characterized the first *paro* began to disintegrate into disparate interests and identities. The Indigenous leaders had been right to note the unequal ratio of *colonos* and *indígenas* employed by the company. But they had exaggerated the extent of this inequality. And while such inequalities could not be understood in abstraction from the colonization of the region, in this case the unequal employment ratio was not primarily the fault of the local mestizo and Afro-descendant population. Rather, it was due first-and-foremost to the racist attitudes of the company management, whose systematic discrimination against the Indigenous population had been one of the principal grievances of the *paro*. The Indigenous leaders also neglected to mention the Indigenous membership of the *comité*, and the involvement of the Indigenous *comunas* of Charapa and Kapáku in the negotiations underway in Auca Central. More fundamentally, their message ignored the lived experience of the *paro* itself, through which the differences they were emphasizing had been transcended in the cut and thrust of a common struggle.

*****

Meanwhile, things were going badly in Auca Central. Far from the backroom stitch up depicted by the president of CONAIE, the representatives of the *paro* were fighting vehemently against an intransigent adversary. In contrast to the negotiations of October 5, when the members of the delegation were slumped in their seats, footage from inside Auca Central shows Darío, Méndez, and Rosa Kapáku on their feet, shouting in the faces of the managers and ministers. The Labor Ministry had once again failed to present the promised report. Instead, they brazenly declared that CGA were not guilty of *tercerización*, without providing any evidence to support this conclusion. At 11pm, after over 12 hours of fruitless remonstrations, the negotiations broke up without agreement, beyond the promise of further negotiations in Quito on October 24.

That was another five days away. The government and the company were playing the long game again, trying to grind down the resolve of the *paro*, while allegedly propagating the rumors about Judith Hidalgo that had been at the heart of the rupture between Dayuma and Inés Arango. These rumors centered on a document circulating on social media that seemed to be signed by Judith and CGA, and which appeared to prove that she had received a bribe from the company. While many were convinced of its authenticity, others argued that such a receipt would hardly exist for a corrupt transaction of this kind and suggested that CGA and the governor had falsified the document in order to engender the division. In the words of a mestizo settler who had participated in many *paros* in the past:

> Inés Arango and Dayuma were united. But the political work of the government, through the governor and the authorities, persuaded them to negotiate separately … These are the tactics that all governments use when they want

> to divide an organized *pueblo*. [And] here, when we are organized, it's a real battle. Here people really do unite.[6]

But despite the successful division of the struggle into two separate factions, the *paro* in Dayuma was stronger than ever, with only public transport allowed to pass the multiple blockades. And instead of having one gang of rebels to deal with, now they had two. On their return to Inés Arango, the Indigenous communities of the parish initiated an independent *paro*, demanding jobs with CGA. They immediately blocked the road to all traffic, including public transport, and entered the oil platforms to shut down the wells. The *paro* was led by the *Huaorani* and *Shuar* communities of the parish, and *Kichwas* and local *colonos* were also involved – around six hundred people in total. Photographs show masked men blocking the road in the rain, amid single-story wooden huts and crumbling concrete walls.[7]

Compared to the *paro* in Dayuma, as Edison Kapáku cheerfully informed me, the *paro* in Inés Arango was "more upheaval, more revolution!"[8] Three truckloads of soldiers were dispatched to open the road, but as they approached the barricade, the jungle around them began to shake with dynamite detonated by *Shuar* renegades hidden in the trees, and the army came under fierce attack from a group of *Huaorani* who forced them to retreat under a barrage of spears. When a local TV crew arrived, the *Huaorani* detained them and confiscated their camera, accusing them of working for the company and threatening to kill them, before releasing them a few hours later. Meanwhile, public buses were hijacked by the *Huaorani* and used as free rebel transport up and down the Savage Road, fueled by diesel stolen from the occupied oil wells.

The *paro* in Dayuma was also continuing to consolidate and intensify. At least eight hundred people now maintained the main barricade, and black plastic tents like the one we had sheltered under during the first *paro* now stretched up the hillside on both sides of the road. Many of the oil wells had run out of fuel, and the uprising was now costing Schlumberger over $1 million a day.[9] It was at this point that the leaders of the *paro* in Dayuma received a tip-off from a soldier that the army had been given an order "from on high," and was finally going to break the blockade. They began preparing to resist the crackdown. Mobile phone images show masked men armed with chainsaws, and according to Edison Kapáku, the *Shuar* had commandeered 26 *motobombas* – motorized fumigation pumps with a spraying range of over 30 feet. These were filled with hot chili sauce, which burns worse than teargas when sprayed into the eyes. Forty gallons of kerosene had been set aside for the manufacture of Molotov cocktails. And barrels of diesel were lined up along the roadside at the entrance to Dayuma, ready to be overturned and ignited as the military passed. The Savage Road would be transformed into a highway of fire.

*****

Dayuma was on the brink of returning to the "civil war" of 2007, when soldiers and renegades engaged in running battles throughout the region. When everything was ready, Edison Kapáku informed Colonel Wilson Tualombo that the *paro* was aware of his planned intervention, and was prepared to resist it, warning him that

> there will be countless deaths. There will be civilian, military and police deaths, and the responsibility will lie with the president of Ecuador. We are not looking for a war, we are looking for our rights. But if you are looking for a war, then a war is what you will find!

Edison then told the colonel that the forces of the *paro* included 40 *Shuar* veterans of the 1998 war with Peru. This was a lie – in fact the only veteran was Santiak, the guy who had been assigned to protect me after my attempted detention by the police and the fake cop during the first *paro*. But these veterans have an unparalleled reputation in the Ecuadorian military for ferocious bravery. When the colonel heard that there would be 40 of them to contend with, "it made his asshole go like this," Edison explained, rapidly squeezing and stretching his fingers to mimic a sphincter flinching in spasmodic terror.[10]

The military intervention was promptly called off, and all attention turned to the negotiations in Quito on the 24th. On the night of the 23rd, three buses made the long journey to the highlands, carrying the representatives of the *comité* and large contingents of the Charapa and Kapáku clans. The negotiations were to be held in the Labor Ministry. But before going there, the delegation staged a demonstration in front of the headquarters of Schlumberger. Smartphone footage shows a group of *Shuar* women and children dancing in the shadows of glass-plated tower blocks, surrounded by workers holding placards accusing Schlumberger of *tercerización*, while the white Quito elite peer out of the tinted windows of their SUVs in gawking incomprehension.

On their arrival at the Labor Ministry, the delegation was received by the vice-minister of labor, along with the sub-secretary of hydrocarbons and the sub-secretary of conflict management (*gestión política*). Finally, it seemed, their cause was being taken seriously. Neither CGA nor Schlumberger were present, and the governor was not in attendance either. But this time, the ministers were not being evasive, and were not shamelessly defending the interests of the two companies. Photographs show them facing the delegation across a table as equals. Marco Kapáku, Rosa Kapáku, and Bolívar Naichap are seated directly opposite the ministers, armed with their spears. The ministers are listening attentively to Enrique Morales, the veteran negotiator of the ABP. According to Darío Rodríguez, Enrique dominated the negotiations, and succeeded in convincing the ministers that CGA was operating illegally, and that Schlumberger was guilty of *tercerización*.[11]

The negotiations resulted in a document entitled "Act of Accords and Commitments between the Works Council and the Central Government," which was signed by the ministers and all members of the delegation. The agreement stated that in exchange for lifting the *paro*, all 1,100 employees of CGA would have their contracts transferred to CPP – the company sub-contracted by Schlumberger in the neighboring oilfield of Shushufindi. Like CGA, CPP was a subsidiary of the Argentinian multinational Techint. But unlike CGA, Schlumberger paid *utilidades* to the employees of CPP. From this point onwards, all the employees in Block 61 would receive the same *utilidades* as those in Shushufindi. The same pay-scale, working hours, and number and quality of meals enjoyed by the CPP employees in Shushufindi would apply to the employees in Block 61. And no worker could be fired or otherwise punished for their participation in the *paro*. Schlumberger, on the other hand, was guilty of *tercerización*, and would be fined accordingly.[12]

It was a total victory! Astonishing! Inconceivable! Nineteen days after the launch of the second *paro*, two months after the uprising in which I had participated, and seven months after the initial failure to pay *utilidades*, the *paro* had achieved its ultimate objective: the expulsion of CGA from Block 61. Footage filmed that night shows a "caravan of struggle" circling ecstatically outside the gates of Auca Central – a high-speed stream of motorbikes, skidding and pulling wheelies, ridden by the renegades, with friends and lovers whooping it up behind. The spiraling headlights, taillights, and smartphone screens mingle with the floodlights of the oil station and the flames of the gas flare to create a kaleidoscopic lightshow playing across the darkened foliage. Over the top of this roaring midnight carnival, an anonymous voice bellows triumphantly through a distorted microphone:

> At this moment, a motorized march is taking place in front of Auca Central! In front of the gates of Block 61! A motorized ritual [performed] by the *compañeros* who have maintained the workers' struggle! This is the voice of the people, the voice of resistance that continues, and that will continue forever! Dayuma will never cease our struggle! ... The labor struggle and the process of resistance live in the blood of everyone who has created this territory![13]

At 5am, the delegation returned from Quito to Dayuma, where the rest of the *paro* had been partying all night in anticipation of their arrival. Once the celebrations were over, the blockade was dismantled, the site was tidied up, the sound system and cooking implements were returned, and everyone slept off their hangovers in preparation for the resumption of work the following day. Meanwhile, a ministerial delegation traveled to the blockade in Inés Arango, which was still underway. The ministers promised that CPP would provide an additional two hundred jobs for the inhabitants of the parish. The road was opened, and by the evening of the 25th the *paro* was finally over.

Or so it seemed. The next morning, the entire workforce was at the *Obrador Central* by 6:30am, ready to complete the paperwork required to make the transition from CGA to CPP. But the camp was deserted. They waited there all day, but no one from CPP showed up, and neither did anyone else. Unsurprisingly, the oil companies were unhappy with the content of the agreement that had been signed in their absence. The following day, representatives of CPP arrived with a contract inferior to the one pertaining to the workers in the Shushufindi field. It was angrily rejected, and the *paro* was instantly resumed. One worker left the scene immediately on his motorbike. He was a poor man with a young family, and he had been a tireless foot-soldier of the *paro*. Other workers say he was distraught at the news that the situation was still unresolved, and had told them that he had no idea how he would continue to put food on the table in the absence of a wage. He was driving fast in the rain when he lost control and collided with an oil tanker. He was dead by the time the ambulance arrived – his head split open and his blood running thick and red into the ditch on the edge of the Savage Road.[14]

The news of his death further strengthened the resolve of the workers, who were already furious at the betrayal of the terms of the agreement by their new employer. This time, almost everyone joined the *paro*, and the road into Dayuma was shut down completely. There were no dances or caravans. Everyone was utterly sick of the situation. This included the government, and possibly even Schlumberger. Until now, Schlumberger had been determined to avoid paying *utilidades* in a context of near bankruptcy generated by the refusal of Ecuador to pay its debts. But in the last couple of weeks, Ecuador had finally cleared most of its $1.1 billion debt to the company and had pledged to pay off the remaining $300 million by the end of November.[15] And now the revenues from ongoing extraction in Block 61 were finally flowing into the company account. The last thing Schlumberger wanted was another *paro* in Dayuma. The next day CPP returned to the *Obrador Central* with a contract offering identical terms to those of Shushufindi. Everyone signed, and work resumed on the expansion of the oil frontier.[16]

*****

The workers were happy. Wages rose, hours improved, overtime was paid, and breakfast was served. CPP even threw a welcome party for them and their families, with free company T-shirts and baseball caps for everyone. And in April, they would finally receive their long-awaited *utilidades*. But the unemployed inhabitants of Block 61 had been forgotten. Many of them had fought long and hard in both *paros*, and yet they had been left with nothing, while the workers – many of whom had not participated in the *paro* and some of whom had actively opposed it – were reaping the benefits of their struggle. Of the two hundred jobs promised to the parish of Inés Arango, only 20 or so materialized. And in Taracoa and El Dorado, the situation was even worse. Inhabitants of all three parishes continued to accuse Judith Hidalgo of working behind the scenes to ensure preferential treatment for the parishioners of Dayuma, and rumors abounded of certain Indigenous leaders and communities doing secret deals with the company to gain access to employment opportunities behind the backs of others.

The outcome was a disintegration of the unity of the *paro* along multiple axes: between workers and the unemployed; between different parishes; between different ethnicities; and between different communities. The company and the state were widely understood to be fomenting these divisions, with the help of specialists trained for such purposes by the hydrocarbon and conflict management ministries, and the "community relations officers" of Schlumberger and CPP – no doubt including Alex Nunes, the skinny-jeaned schemer who had so miserably failed in his attempt to discourage and divide the initial uprising. This time the strategy had been more concerted and successful. But far from neutralizing the insurrectional tendencies of the region, it unintentionally triggered an explosion of small, fragmented *paros*, as each individual parish, ethnicity, and community sought to replicate the success of the *paro* in Dayuma.

The shitstorm began almost immediately. In November 2017, unemployed workers from the parish of Taracoa accused CPP of excluding them in favor of workers from other parts of the country. Once again, the *Obrador Central* was closed down, although this time without the support of its employees. On the fifth day of the shutdown, the renegades responded to police repression by attacking a patrol car, smashing its windows and slashing its tires, before setting it alight. Four people were arrested and publicly denounced as terrorists by the governor of Orellana, before being released without charge. The *paro* concluded the next day, with a guarantee of 30 new jobs for the inhabitants of Taracoa.[17]

The success of the *paro* in Taracoa inspired the *comuna* of Kapáku to launch a *paro* of their own, demanding more jobs for its members, and improved compensation for the construction of a second oil platform on their territory. They shut down production at the first platform, which had now come onstream. When the police arrived to evict them, they attacked them with spears and stones and forced them to retreat. The *paro* lasted a week, and gained 14 new jobs for the *comuna*, in addition to a water pump, a basketball court, an access road and a communal meeting house.[18]

And if a solitary *Shuar comuna* could achieve such gains, then the *Kichwa* could do the same. In January 2018, the *Kichwa comuna* of Rumbipamba, located south of Dayuma along the *Vía Auca*, launched a *paro* to protest the dismissal of a member of their community by CPP. They blocked the entrance to an oil platform being constructed on their land, prevented the circulation of CPP vehicles on the *Vía Auca*, and confiscated an excavator belonging to CPP. The terms of its return were simple. The worker who had been fired was an excavator driver. If CPP wanted their excavator back, they were going to have to give the excavator driver his job back. Three days later he was reinstated, along with a commitment from the company to provide 15 further jobs for the *comuneros* of Rumbipamba.[19]

Now things started kicking off everywhere. Over the next few months, CPP was confronted with further *paros* in the mestizo communities of Valle Hermoso (Beautiful Valley) and Vencedores del Oriente (Victors of the East), as well as the Afro-descendant community of Ciudad Blanca and the entire parish of El Dorado. Meanwhile, the wave of *paros* was spreading to other oilfields in the region run by other foreign companies. The Belorussian company Petrobell faced *paros* in the *colono* community of Esfuerzo Amazónico (Amazonian Striving) and in the *Kichwa* community of Rio Tiputini. The *colono* community of Pindo Central launched a *paro* against the Brazilian company Petrorivas. And the Chinese company PetroOriental was confronted with *paros* in Santa Rosa and Rodrigo Borja in the region of El Pindo – the sites of some of the fiercest conflicts during the "civil war" of 2007.

Employment was the central demand of the majority of these *paros*, and in most cases they were successful in obtaining at least a handful of jobs for their communities. This was made possible by the boom that was underway across the region.

CPP was taking on more workers as the expansion of Block 61 accelerated, and new wells were being drilled in many of the surrounding blocks. But the jobs that were provided were always fewer than had been promised, and the workers were usually fired after three months – the limit of the probation period within which a worker can be dismissed for no reason, without the company incurring redundancy payments or facing legal challenge. In February 2018, a group of unemployed workers from across the four parishes of Block 61 marched to the office of the governor to demand that he intervene to address the situation. Instead, Colon Malla doggedly defended the hire-and-fire policy of CPP and the other oil companies. The unemployed workers responded by organizing a demonstration in Coca, demanding the dismissal of the governor due to his repeated betrayal of the inhabitants of the region, and his flagrant subordination to the interests of the oil companies. The next day, Colon Malla was summoned to Quito, and removed from his post.[20]

*****

Uprisings were spreading like wildfire along the Savage Road, and it was only a matter of time before the *Huaorani* got involved. Following their attempted lynching of Judith Hidalgo in the coliseum in Dayuma, and their leading role in the subsequent *paro* in Inés Arango, the *Huaorani* had retreated back into their communities, accusing the *Shuar* and *Kichwa* of treachery and double-dealing. Toward the end of March 2018, however, the *Huaorani* community of Obatawe launched a *paro* in a block operated by the state oil company Petroamazonas. Obatawe is located several miles down a gravel track toward the far southern end of the *Vía Auca*, and the block in question lies within its territory. The community is led by Miguel Obatawe, who is widely believed to be a hitman working for illegal logging crews operating in the Intangible Zone, where such activities are banned. The loggers allegedly pay him to secure their activities in the region, by murdering members of the *Tagaeri* and *Taromenane* who are living there in "voluntary isolation."[21]

The community of Obatawe had originally wanted to create an oil company to exploit the block themselves. When this plan failed, they created a construction company, with which they hoped to win the contract with Petroamazonas to build the oil platform. Instead, the contract was granted to a Quito-based company, which signed an agreement with Obatawe to the effect that all unskilled labor and basic services such as food and local transport would be provided by the community company.[22] This agreement had not been honored. The community demanded a dialogue with Petroamazonas, who promised to send the new governor and a ministerial delegation to resolve the situation immediately. They didn't show up. By this point, the first platform was already pumping crude, which was hauled out by tanker, and a second platform was under construction. The inhabitants of Obatawe felled trees across the access road to block the departure of tankers and construction vehicles, and then descended on the oil platforms armed with spears and machetes. Workers, drivers, and security guards were stripped naked and sent running for their lives.

The next day, four truckloads of soldiers and three busloads of riot police arrived to break the *paro*. They assembled on the road at the entrance to the community, where they were confronted by a group of around 30 *Huaorani*. Despite being massively outnumbered, the *Huaorani* immediately launched an attack, smashing the cops and soldiers in the head with their spears, and shattering their shields with their machetes. The security forces were driven back, before regrouping at the edge of town. The ensuing standoff was captured by a local cable news report. A group of seven or eight women are on the frontline, with a larger group of men in the background. One of the women addresses the camera: "If the military attacks we will kill them! Because our *pueblo* will not allow anyone to crush us! No-one! No-one! Police nor military! We are going to kill!" She chops her arm downward to express this intent. The clip then cuts to Miguel Obatawe. His Spanish is rough and ready, but the gist of his message is not difficult to grasp: "Suddenly temper can be lost, and the one who kills is me … Here soldiers arrive, I kill immediately. If they push me I kill at once."

News then comes that more soldiers have indeed arrived – a rifle squad has just been dropped by helicopter onto one of the oil platforms in Obatawe territory. The women immediately disappear in that direction, while the men maintain the standoff with the cops and soldiers at the entrance to their community. What happened next was described to me by Diana Obatawe, one of Miguel's daughters and a well-known *Huaorani* leader in her own right. Diana had hooked up with Méndez, the mestizo leader of the *comité*, during the second *paro*, in one of several liaisons inspired by the passionate political proceedings. Méndez took me to her home, where she recalled the events to the rampant laughter of her sisters.

When they reached the platform, the women ambushed the soldiers who had just landed, and took them hostage. The helicopter soon returned with another squad of soldiers, but the women pelted it with spears as it neared the ground and prevented it from landing. One of the captured soldiers tried to pull a pistol, but they smacked him around the head with their spears before he could do so. They tied the soldiers up and stripped them of their teargas canisters, before returning to Obatawe, where they launched the teargas at the cops and soldiers on the frontline. The forces of law and order scattered in chaos, while the *Huaorani* celebrated their victory, before accidentally turning the teargas against themselves. Then they marched the kidnapped soldiers out of their territory, "spanking their asses" with the flat sides of their machetes, "as if they were little children." The moment was caught on film by the local news channel: eight soldiers in full military fatigues are walking hurriedly down a gravel road, clutching their rifles and darting furtive glances left and right. They are pursued by the women swinging their spears and machetes and shouting a merciless series of derogatory epithets, while the men of Obatawe line the sides of the road. A dog brings up the rear of the procession.

*****

The *paro* in Obatawe was finally resolved in early April, 11 days after it had begun, with the promise of 14 additional jobs for the community and the contracting of their company for the construction of the second platform of the local oilfield. It was another famous victory in this new era of insurrection on the Savage Road. As in the golden age of the *paros* over a decade previously, the entire region was ablaze with blockades and uprisings. And in a few days' time the payment of *utilidades* would fall due. The failure of CGA to make this payment one year previously had started the smoldering discontent that had been ignited on the day of my arrival in Dayuma back in August 2017, and that was now raging out of control. If CPP were to fail to make the payment this time, under these conditions, the *Obrador Central* would surely be burned to the ground. They had no choice. They made the payout. And they paid out big. 1,100 workers received a base rate of $14,000, with an additional $4,000 per dependent. The average worker was getting a windfall of over $20,000, and payouts of $30,000 or $40,000 were not uncommon. The more children you had, the better, and if husband and wife both worked for the company, then they doubled their money. There was talk of one *Shuar* couple who had really hit the jackpot. They both worked for CPP, and they had 12 children. Apparently, they received over $120,000!

I returned to Dayuma four months after the payment of *utilidades*, and it was a different town. The Hotel Guerrero was adding another floor and building a restaurant, and the entire hotel had been refurbished. The shack where I used to get my cheap cups of instant coffee was now a seafood place with glossy menus. While I was there, a scruffy mestizo oil worker ambled in with a miniature pedigree dog in a frilly little frock – the favored pet of the Quito elite. The place I used to get breakfast had also been upgraded, and a new hotel was being built in the gorge that ran beneath the roadside. Many of the workers had invested their cash in new houses, cars, motorbikes, and water pumps. Some had opened bars and restaurants. Some had bought land or set up small businesses in the oil services industry. And not a few had blown the lot in the bars and brothels of Coca. Four of them were said to have burned through $8,000 this way together on the first night alone.

The workers had won the war. But their economic victory turned out to be their political defeat. Schlumberger had done everything in their power to avoid the payment of *utilidades*, and every one of their strategies had failed. But it was the very payment itself that finally reestablished their hegemony. Now everyone was desperate to work for CPP, in the hope of getting in on the next disbursement of *utilidades*. And now no one dared to launch a *paro* to demand employment, in case it might result in them being blacklisted by the company. By this point, CPP had made clear that there was a heavy price to be paid for involvement in a *paro*. On November 24, 2017, less than a month after the transition from CGA to CPP, Darío and Méndez had been fired, along with 13 other leading figures in the *comité*. They had been unemployed ever since. Over the course of the subsequent weeks, almost every other employee who had played a prominent role in the *paro* was dismissed, including Pedro, the pug-faced guy with the mohawk who expelled the *sapos*, and Tilapia and Barberan, whose detention had triggered the initial uprising. This was a clear violation of the amnesty included in the agreement that had brought the *paro* to an end. But the other workers kept their heads down and focused on securing their own *utilidades*. Even Olger Naichap, the firebrand hero of the first *paro*, and one of only three surviving leaders of the *comité*, bit his tongue and counted his blessings that his own job had been spared. The vacancies in the leadership were filled by obedient servants of the company managers, who warned them that they would be fired if they ever dared to associate with Darío and Méndez again.

This was explained to me during a meeting with the two other survivors of the leadership cull. They had seen me walking through Dayuma but had not dared to approach me on the street, in case one of the company spies was watching. Instead, they came to find me in my hotel, and asked if we could meet somewhere else, so they could tell me what was happening behind the scenes. I suggested going for a drink in Coca, but this was also too dangerous in their opinion – CPP had *sapos* everywhere. Instead, they invited me to one of their houses the next evening – a wooden hut in a hollow beneath the road in El Dorado, with a huge new sound system and an enormous flat-screen TV purchased with their payout. We hunkered down in the porch with some beers, out of sight of the road. It was the same old shit, they said. Apart from the payment of *utilidades*, the shift from CGA to CPP had been a sham – a change of uniform and nothing more. With the exception of the operations manager Esteban García, who had fled the country following his kidnapping ordeal, the same managers were still in place, and the case against the ones involved in the WhatsApp murder plot had come to nothing.[23] Meanwhile, after initial improvements, the old forms of exploitation and abuse were returning: 12-hour working days with no paid overtime, the denigration of Indigenous employees, and the replacement of local labor with passive, compliant workers from elsewhere.

No one dared to challenge the company on any of these issues. To do so would be to risk dismissal, and to lose their share in the next round of *utilidades*. They admitted this to me, with their eyes turned to the ground. On the way back to Dayuma, in a big red pickup truck also bought with one of their payouts, they spoke of Darío and Méndez with great respect and affection: "It has to be acknowledged that they were true leaders. They fought until the very end." But if they saw them on the street, they would shake hands with them and move on without a word.[24]

The rage and revolt of the *paro* had been replaced by fear and loathing. Walking around Dayuma, I could sense the animosity and distrust seething below the surface. And I was sure that some of it was directed against me. Almost everyone had sold out in some way, and they didn't want me hanging around, asking questions and causing trouble. After all, either I was a spy for CPP, or I was an enemy of CPP, and either way I was bad news for them. One evening I met up with Rosa Kapáku, the most bellicose of all the *Shuar* women during the *paro*, who had participated in the kidnapping of Esteban García, and had emasculated Wilmer Armas in the coliseum. She was waiting in the shadow of a doorway on the corner of a side street. Like the surviving representatives of the *comité*, she did not want to be seen with me in public in case word got back to CPP. She had just finished her shift, after securing a three-month post with the company in the aftermath of the *paro* in Kapáku territory. She knew that she would be laid off once the three months were up, and that she would not get any *utilidades*. But Rosa was a single mother, and she could not risk this rare opportunity for a monthly minimum wage. We moved from the street into the relative safety of my hotel room, where she told me that her brother Marco's house had been burned down by CPP, as punishment for his role in the *paros*. I said that I would like to visit them in Kapáku. But she asked me not to come. "If they see you there, they might fire all of us," she said. "Now the company has us like this," she added, and made a motion like the wringing of a wet rag.

Later that evening, I headed into town to find some food. It was Sunday night, and everyone was getting wasted in whatever way they could afford. While the workers lived it up with the spoils of their victory, the unemployed continued to struggle for survival, and beneath the veneer of shiny things purchased with the payout, Dayuma was as impoverished and alienated as ever. Groups of men were gathered around bottles of cheap spirits in the darkness on the edges of the road. Someone blundered past me ranting to himself, ripped his shirt off his back and threw it in the gutter. Another man approached me, with skinny ribs, stuck-out ears, and a missing tooth. Tigrillo! The guy on the back of the motorbike who had saved me from the fake cop. One of the most delinquent renegades of the entire *paro*, who had "dawned" every night and been on the frontline every day. I had been told that he had been fired, and that he had not been seen or heard of since. And here he was! I greeted him with a laugh and an embrace. But he wasn't laughing, and he didn't greet me in return. He was silent and sweating, and he stared at me with vacant eyes. Then he muttered something under his breath. I asked him to repeat it. He needed three dollars. It was the first time anyone here had asked me for cash. I was taken aback, and I heard myself telling him that I didn't have any change. Before I could say anything else, he turned and stumbled on down the street.

It was getting late, and most of the restaurants were closed. But a barbecue place was still open at the bottom of the hill. I ducked inside. It was empty except for a table at the back, where Diana Obatawe and her sisters were getting drunk with three oil men from Petroamazonas. I sat down with them, and the bottles kept coming thick and fast. Petroamazonas was picking up the tab, they explained, and the recent conflict between the two parties seemed to have been forgotten. There was a lot of lewd humor and double entendre, and Diana was getting on particularly well with one of the men. He leaned over to me, laughing, and told me that "Diana loves me one minute and has a spear against my neck the next!" Everyone was wrecked by this point, and the same guy started giving me tips on how to deal with Diana's father, the volatile alleged hitman of Obatawe: "Miguel used to be much more aggressive," he confided, "But he still loves whores, and if you sit him down in front of a porn movie then he's happy."

They were still going strong when I staggered out of there a couple hours later. It had been a difficult experience for me to grasp. When I described the scene to an outreach worker who had worked closely with the *Huaorani* over many years, he explained it in concise terms: "People are looking for ways to survive and adapt, and they get infected by the spirit of oil, which is very dark."[25] These were the kinds of situations in which consciences were bought, and divisions were sown. The guys from Petroamazonas who were buying the drinks were playing the same game as those negotiating with communities on behalf of CPP. They were all dedicated to paying people off and turning leaders, communities, and ethnicities against each other, in order to guard against the kind of unity that had emerged in the *paro*. Back in Coca, I spoke with Diocles Zambrano, a grizzled old *colono*, self-educated human rights activist, and veteran of countless *paros*. From his point of view, the spontaneous unity of the *paro* had not been a fleeting illusion, but was an expression of the common relation to capital shared by the communities of the region:

> [The *paro* in Dayuma] was a single group. Because in reality it *is* a single group. *Huao*, *Kichwa* or *Shuar*, apart from the small traditions that each group possesses – and that the mestizos also possess – in reality there isn't much difference. And the moment they unite [against the company] is the moment they realize that they're all on the same side, that they shouldn't be fighting amongst themselves. But that harmony doesn't last long when a so-called "professional" comes and tells [one group] "No, you shouldn't join with them because you are superior to them, and they have no business to be involved in this." But that's [only] what he says when he's with them. When he's with the other group he says "The thing is that you shouldn't join with [the first group] because they're trying to sabotage [you]. They're trying to take what I'm supposed to be giving to you." [And so on,] until all the groups end up divided.[26]

According to Diocles, this was precisely how the companies and the government had operated to break the initial unity of the *paro* in Dayuma. This opinion was shared by many of the more battle-hardened observers of the *paro*. In the words of one *Kichwa* leader:

> There was unity. But then they separated into different groups. There were accusations against the leaders, accusations against the parish authorities. The company used some very technical people to weaken the entire group. In other words, the company saw that everyone was united and sent people to divide them. They created an internal division, and the strength was lost.[27]

This sense of unity – of *universal humanity* – had defined the initial uprising. But the strategy of division had been devastatingly effective. By the time I returned to Dayuma less than one year later, everyone was at each other's throats. The parishioners from Inés Arango believed that Judith Hidalgo was cutting deals with the company in favor of the parishioners of Dayuma, who accused her of selling their jobs to people from other parts of the country.[28] The *Kichwa* accused the *Shuar* and the *Huaorani* of signing a deal with CPP behind their backs, while the *Shuar* and the *Huaorani* claimed that the *Kichwa* were working for the government to subvert the *paro*. The *Shuar* of Kapáku said the *Shuar* of Charapa were trying to profit independently from the *paro*, while the *Shuar* of Charapa claimed that Judith Hidalgo had tried to bribe them to abandon it.

The list of rumors and counter-rumors was endless, and the resulting fractures spread and multiplied, to the point of shattering the integrity of individual families. Even Marco and Edison Kapáku, the brothers at the center of the first *paro*, whose leadership had been so vital at so many crucial moments in the struggle, were now estranged from one another, each accusing the other of collusion with the enemy. It was impossible to get to the bottom of what was really going on. Not because there was no truth to be deciphered, but because what was *really* going on was this bottomless ambiguity itself – an impenetrable fog of suspicion and innuendo, deliberately conjured by the "professionals," in dealings like the drunken encounter I had witnessed between the women of Obatawe and the oil men.

And while everyone was wallowing in this morass of distrust and paranoia, and scrambling over one another to get a piece of the next payout, Schlumberger quietly continued to execute its systematic theft of their natural resources. The extravagance of the *utilidades*, which represented a combined total of just three percent of Schlumberger's annual profits from Block 61, only served to indicate the obscene quantities of wealth that the company was extracting from the region.[29] Things were looking up these days for Schlumberger. It had weathered the storm of the oil crash, thanks to the dismissal of 70,000 workers worldwide in under three years, combined with the brutal levels of exploitation implemented by its subcontractors in places like Dayuma. Ecuador had cleared its debts to the company, and profit margins and stock prices were on the rise again.[30] In a couple years from now, the expansion of Block 61 would be complete, and Schlumberger could rid itself of this unruly workforce, and settle back to pump the oil and count the cash in peace.

*****

On my last day in Dayuma, I wandered up the hill out of town, past the humming activity of the *Obrador Central* and the ghostly silence of the site of the blockade. I headed off the Savage Road onto a track that led to an oil platform in the jungle, where a solitary gas flare roared proudly in the sunlight, like a secluded shrine to some demonic god. Or a monument to the insurgent universality that had scorched through this place like a passing comet. I stood there for a while, watching the flames surge and blossom against the clear blue sky.

7 The Insurgent Universal

What are the political implications of story I have told? At the level of cold hard facts, you could argue that it doesn't amount to much. Just another heroic tale of insurrectional failure. Another brave struggle against impossible odds, in which the combined forces of state and capital gradually crushed the life out of a grass-roots rebellion. The workers could claim some remarkable victories: they had expelled a multinational company from their territory; they had deposed the corrupt governor of their province; and they had won the battle to be paid what they were due. But while CGA had been thrown out, the same corporation remained under the name of CPP. The same managers were still in place, and the same abuses soon returned. Schlumberger still ran the show, and foreign capital still kept its fat cut of the oil ripped from beneath their feet. And what did the workers care? It's not as if they were militant communists committed to seizing the means of production, smashing the state, and overthrowing capitalism. They were just a bunch of local roughnecks who were sick of being screwed over and decided to take matters into their own hands. The only thing they were after was their share of the oil rents. And once they got it, they were happy. The end.

Perhaps. But that isn't what really matters here. The political significance of the struggle cannot be grasped by the sober assessment of its stated motives, or the calculated comparison of its victories and defeats. It lies instead in the fleeting emergence of a transcendent dimension that blazed through all the murky chaos of the uprising, like early morning sunlight through cloud-laden jungle. Suddenly, an extractive frontier configured by bitter colonial legacies, in thrall to the power of transnational capital, and scarred by the socioecological devastation of the global oil industry, was illuminated by an insurgent universality, in which the racial, ethnic, and cultural divisions that marked the region miraculously ceased to matter. *Shuar*, *Kichwa*, *Huaorani*, or mestizo; Black, white, brown, or albino; woman or man; worker, peasant, or unemployed – everyone picked up a spear and joined the battle, as if moved to do so by an unseen force far greater than themselves.

This motley crew was united by a common material relation to capital. And this commonality did not need to be explained to them by Marxist intellectuals bent on their indoctrination. It was rendered starkly evident by the conditions of super-exploitation to which all workers of the region were being submitted by a single multinational company seeking to maximize its local profits in the

DOI: 10.4324/9781003345879-7

context of a global oil crisis. They all boarded the same bus at the same brutal hour of the morning. They all missed the same non-existent breakfast. They all ate the same rotten lunch. They all sweated the same bullets. They all suffered the same exhaustion. They all got ripped off in the same way. Nothing could be more obvious. That is why, when the two strike leaders were seized by the cops on the instructions of the company, the *Shuar* outside the gates didn't dismiss them as mestizos – as members of a foreign invading culture. Instead, they treated them as comrades – as fellow human beings fighting on the same side in a seemingly impossible struggle against the vast amorphous monster of multinational capital. And as comrades they stormed the gates to seize the manager in revenge. When Bolívar Naichap called on those around him to tear off their shirts and raise their spears, he did not limit his call to his fellow *Shuar*, or to other Indigenous nationalities. Instead, he proclaimed that everyone was Indigenous. Not in the sense of a shared racial phenotype or common cultural tradition – for none existed. But as a singular embodiment of the insurgent universal.

This universality did not imply the erasure of all differences beneath a Westernized homogeneity. After all, the renegades were not all designated as white or mestizo, but as Indigenous, and this designation was not made by a Western ideologue, but by an Indigenous leader. This collective assumption of a shared Indigenous identity became a recurrent rallying cry of the uprising, without blinding the rebels to the significance of the very real differences that existed between them. The denigration reserved for the Indigenous employees by the racist company bosses was one of the principal grievances identified by all workers – Indigenous, Black, and mestizo. And the specific traditions of the Indigenous communities participating in the uprising were accentuated in the everyday rituals of resistance – not as exclusive assertions of ethnic particularism, but as joyful contributions to a common struggle, in which mestizos also increasingly participated. When Edison Kapáku grabbed the mic and began to shout above the *Shuar* music and dances, his distorted aphorisms did not invoke his own ancestral traditions. Instead, they celebrated the collective creation of a new world in which "we are united," and where "we are not what we were before."

This new world was not a blueprint imposed by dogmatic prophets of historical progress, in which Indigenous traditions would be sacrificed on the altar of a Eurocentric modernity. It was staged directly in the here and now, by the Indigenous inhabitants of the *Vía Auca* themselves, along with their Black, white, and mestizo comrades. The universality that they collectively embodied should not be understood in essentialist terms, as a positive attribute of the human condition or a common material substrate underlying all cultures. Rather, it is defined by a shared experience of alienation. For the motley crew of the Savage Road, this experience was generated by the diverse processes of dispossession that had forced them all onto this remote extractive frontier, where they now found themselves collectively entangled in the alien machinations of global capital accumulation. This common experience was expressed in the lyrics of the *Shuar* folksong over which Edison Kapáku bellowed his messages of revolutionary unity: "I wander far away in another land/ A land I have never known/ I am here, dancing to this music/ I have come from another land and now I am here." It is a form of commonality that is not rooted in feeling at home in a shared culture but grounded in what Buck-Morss describes as a mutual sense of "not being at home in the world, [which] gives rise to a common humanity without the prejudice of personal belonging."[1]

The universal dimension of the *paro* was thus embodied in the spontaneous dynamics of its everyday practice, which flourished within the rupture that the struggle tore into the stable fabric of the status quo. Like the medieval peasantry of Mikhail Bakhtin's carnival, for a few days the renegades "celebrated temporary liberation from the prevailing truth and from the established order" and entered "the utopian realm of ... freedom, equality and abundance."[2] The *freedom* of being delivered from the dictatorship of wage labor and placed in control of their own time – and the outcome of the negotiations ensured that they got paid for every day! The *abundance* of three good meals a day, plus truckloads of bread and fruit, vats of coffee, and sneaky blasts of *aguardiente.* All set to music and filled with singing and dancing – and all for free! And the *equality* asserted by the performance of a world turned upside down, which repeatedly revealed the absence of any natural social order: responding to the detention of their comrades by kidnapping the company manager, forcing the corrupt governor to endure a symbolic spearing, and spanking their captive soldiers' assess with the flat sides of their machetes.

These fantastical inversions of the established power structure were only fleeting, and they could even be accused of ultimately reinforcing the structure that they seemed to subvert, by providing light relief from the rituals of everyday oppression that were soon to be resumed. But that would be to underestimate the volatile fusion of rage and delight with which they were performed. Insurgent universality dwells in what Badiou calls this "collective evental passion ... the thrilling sense of an abrupt alteration in the relationship between the possible and the impossible."[3] This passion is reserved for those who throw themselves across the line dividing the world of hegemonic order from that of its insurrectional negation. The ones who go over the Edge, as Hunter S. Thompson would say, beyond which lies a liminal dimension in which "national and cultural identities are suspended, and unity is the consequence, not of who you are, but rather of what you do."[4]

Insurgent universality thus emerges on the jagged edges of worlds: the spatial limit of the extractive frontier that both sustains and subverts the imperial centers of global capital; the temporal rupture of the uprising that punches a hole through the brittle structures of state power; and the experiential edge of collectively crossing the line that marks the legal and normative boundaries of the established socioeconomic order. As such, it constitutes a dimension of subaltern political actuality, the affirmation of which is entirely consistent with the decolonial injunction to ground theory in the practices of subaltern subjects. This implies that, if it is to remain consistent with its own methodological principles and political commitments, the decolonial critique of extractive capital should reach beyond the dichotomy of Eurocentric universalism and an Indigenous pluriverse, and embrace insurgent universality as both a distinct conceptual dimension, and an alternative living reality with profound emancipatory potential.

That, at least, is my take on the story. Unfortunately, it is unlikely to be an interpretation with which many decolonial scholars would agree. Reflecting on the response of "the academic critics of Eurocentrism" to her argument for the existence of a universal humanity revealed by the slave revolt in Haiti, Buck-Morss recalls that her "decentering of the legacy of Western modernity was applauded." However, her "goal of salvaging modernity's universal intent, rather than calling for a plurality of alternative modernities" was roundly opposed on the grounds that "for some, the very suggestion of resurrecting the project of universal history from the ashes of modern metaphysics appeared tantamount to collusion with Western imperialism."[5] The debate has since moved on, and the notion of the pluriverse has largely replaced that of alternative modernities in postcolonial and decolonial circles. But if anything, the opposition to universality has only intensified. This is particularly the case when it is invoked from the embodied positionality of someone like myself. From the perspective of the decolonial theorist Walter Mignolo, for example, my identity necessarily precludes me from claiming any such experience of unity, due to an "irreducible epistemic colonial difference" between my culture and those of the Indigenous communities involved in the uprising on the Savage Road. To the extent that "a white body in Western Europe" such as my own could hope to understand a situation such as the one in which I participated, Mignolo insists, "that understanding would be rational and intellectual, not experiential."[6]

There is no doubt that my position in the uprising was immensely privileged in many ways. Unlike the renegades, I was not fighting to feed my family. Unlike them, I slept in a hotel on most nights of the struggle. And unlike them, I was free to escape to Western Europe when it suited me to do so. And yet despite all this, once I had crossed the line enough times to win their trust, I was acknowledged as a fellow human being fighting on the same side. As Tomba has observed of such situations: "The revolutionary rupture … is what constitutes insurgent universality … By suspending the present order and all means of belonging, anyone can be on the side of the insurgents, thereby running the risk of not belonging to one's own privileges."[7] My inclusion in this collective suspension of belonging was arguably confirmed by the rescue mission that culminated with the *Shuar* leader forcing the fake cop and his police henchmen to release me. Afterwards we laughed at my whiteness, and the fact that my fear had made me "more pallid than ever." Did this joke rest on the irreconcilable nature of our racial and cultural differences? Or were we able to laugh about these differences because they no longer mattered?

It of course remains an open question if the insurgent universal was ever really present on the Savage Road. The *paro* was certainly only a minor example of the phenomenon, the contours of which only falteringly and sporadically emerged in the chaotic rush of events I have described. Perhaps its appearance was nothing more than a spectral delusion projected onto reality by my own unconscious Eurocentric assumptions. It seems to me, however, that the response to this question should be based on a careful consideration of the case itself, and not on the theoretical rejection of the possibility of insurgent universality in advance. The danger of the latter approach is that those subaltern struggles that do not conform to the decolonial vision of the pluriverse are rendered conceptually unviable, and thus politically invisible. This would violate a guiding principle of decolonial theory: to ground itself in the lived reality of subaltern struggles themselves. Indeed, the dissident decolonial theorist Silvia Rivera Cusicanqui has challenged Mignolo and other prominent decolonial intellectuals on precisely this basis. According to Rivera Cusicanqui, the conceptual apparatus of mainstream decolonial theory "entangles and paralyzes their objects of study: the Indigenous and African-descended people with whom these academics believe they are in dialogue," and "enthrones within the academy a limited and illusory discussion regarding modernity and decolonization, without paying attention to the internal dynamics of the subalterns."[8]

Furthermore, as Asad Haider has argued in his affirmation of insurgent universality, the categorical denial of the possibility of universal experience threatens to reproduce a "separatist ideology [that] prevents the construction of unity among the marginalized, the kind of unity that could actually overcome their marginalization."[9] Over the course of the uprising on the Savage Road, the Ecuadorian state ran through an extensive repertoire of repressive and divisionary tactics: detaining strike leaders and sending in the army; dispatching ex-rebels to sweet-talk the renegades; infiltrating the *paro* with spies to spread distrust and paranoia; repeatedly betraying promises and rescheduling negotiations; and imposing multiple forms of division – between good and bad workers, town and *paro*, blockade and countermarch. But despite all this, the uprising continued to grow in strength. Its unity was only broken by the deployment of divisions based on racial and ethnic differences. These divisions were introduced by the representatives of regional and national Indigenous social movements who sought to seize control of the struggle from outside. The key moment came when Jaime Vargas of CONAIE addressed a restive crowd in the coliseum in Dayuma, and encouraged them to identify not as workers against capital, but as *indígenas* against the local mestizo and Afro-descendant population. This division was quickly seized on by the state. Working closely with the company, and using the promised bonanza of the *utilidades* to spread offers of privilege and rumors of treachery, the government began turning ethnic groups against each other. First *indígenas* against mestizos. Then *Shuar* against *Kichwa* against *Huaorani*. And finally, community against community, family against family, brother against brother. The unintended outcome was an explosion of fragmented *paros*, in which each group sought to grab what it could for itself. But these protests were small and weak and easily placated. And they were no longer illuminated by the insurgent universal. State and capital had won. And they had done so through the creation of a pluriverse.

As Haider concludes, insurgent universality "does not demand emancipation solely for those who share my identity but for everyone ... Every compromise of *this* kind of universality ... [has] led back to the particularism of the existing order."[10] Against such particularism, the spontaneous experience of solidarity among diverse cultures, races, and ethnicities that briefly flourished on the Savage Road resonates with Jodi Dean's definition of comradeship as

> a political relation that shifts us away … from presuppositions of unique particularity … It concerns rather the sameness that comes from being on the same side in a political struggle. In this sense, the comrade is liberated from the determinations of specificity, freed by the common political horizon.[11]

And yet, despite its transcendence of the politics of identity, insurgent universality does not exhaust difference. On the contrary, it tends to assume the particular form of the most excluded element of the false universalism that it opposes. As Žižek has noted, "The paradox is that there is no *Universal* proper without … an out-of-joint entity presenting/manifesting itself as the stand-in for the Universal."[12] This was the role played by Indigenous identity in the uprising on the Savage Road – as the most marginalized element of a frontier proletariat confronting the false universalism of multinational capital, which symbolically embodied insurgent universality through its articulation of the collective battle cry: "We are all Indigenous!" This book has sought to add to the subterranean history of such expressions of universal humanity, as an affirmation of its existence on the extractive frontier, and as a contribution to what Buck-Morss calls "the storehouse of human possibility."[13] But regardless of such historical records, the world will continue to be disrupted by fleeting moments of insurgent universality, as a latent potentiality sustained by the system it opposes, which is always on the verge of leaping into flames.

*****

It began again, as it always does, with a random spark. On October 1, 2019, the Ecuadorian president, Lenín Moreno, announced a series of free market reforms under the nondescript title of "Decree 883." In return for a $4.2 billion loan from the IMF, the government would liberalize trade and capital flows, deregulate the labor market and eliminate the subsidy on diesel and gasoline, which had been in place for almost 40 years. These reforms would come into force in two days' time. They were justified as the price that had to be paid to finally return the nation to fiscal health after the profligate corruption of the Correa regime. But if there was one thing that the Ecuadorian popular classes resented even more than profligate corruption, it was mealy-mouthed politicians placing the cost of economic adjustment squarely on the shoulders of the poor. The most egregious element of the reforms in this regard was the removal of the fuel subsidy, which had long functioned to keep public transport affordable, and peasant agriculture competitive. More to the point, from the perspective of the historically marginalized population of the Ecuadorian Amazon, the fuel subsidy was the only meaningful benefit they had ever received from the state in exchange for the vast petroleum resources that had been sucked out of the region for almost half a century. In the words of a rebel priest based in Coca, everyone was already "up to their balls (*hasta los huevos*). They'd had enough of policies, of politicians, of dialogues, of two-facedness, of corruption. They'd had as much as they could take. They had nowhere left to go."[14]

With the exception of the Ecuadorian representatives of the global business elite and their most shameless bootlickers, the rest of the country felt exactly the same way. Within hours of Moreno's announcement, the national transport unions had joined with other unions and Indigenous movements to announce a nationwide *paro*, which would begin on Thursday, October 3, to coincide with the implementation of the reforms. But Moreno pressed ahead with his plan. The decree came into force, along with a State of Emergency in preparation for the anticipated unrest. Fuel prices doubled overnight, and the bus and taxi unions brought the nation to a standstill. Roadblocks were installed on highways up and down the country, and the Quito international airport was blockaded, leading to its partial shutdown. Yet the very next day, the leaders of the transport unions announced that they had reached an agreement with the government. In return for the raising of restrictions on bus fares and taxi charges, they had accepted the reforms and were calling off the strike. They were siding with the state, and washing their hands of the struggle.[15]

Moreno might have thought that he had gotten away with it. But the Indigenous movements and the other unions were enraged by their betrayal, and their indignation was shared by a population whose survival strategies depended on the fuel subsidy. At this point, CONAIE decided to take matters into their own hands. In marked contrast to the divisive role that he had played in the *paro* on the Savage Road, Jaime Vargas now saw the necessity of building a united movement of *indígenas* and mestizos, peasants and workers. Together with the leading labor unions of the nation, CONAIE announced the formation of the Unitary Collective (*Colectivo Unitario*), which pledged to continue and intensify the *paro*.

Plans were laid over the weekend, while the blockades around the country remained in place. By the morning of Monday, October 7, 20,000 members of Indigenous communities from across the highlands were marching toward Quito. They did not come in peace. On the way, they ransacked the vast plastic greenhouses of the global flower industry, which fill the hills and valleys around the city. They shut down a major paper mill and raided an industrial dairy. They seized control of the governor's office in the town of Guaranda and placed the Governorship of the city of Tungurahua under siege. There were reports of riots and looting in cities throughout the highlands and along the coast, and before the marchers could reach Quito, the impoverished urban youth had already descended from the favelas that cling to the mountainsides on the outskirts of the city, and were burning army vehicles, trashing government ministries, and vandalizing the National Assembly.[16]

It was an ominous panorama for Lenín Moreno. Popular uprisings had deposed three prior presidents in 1997, 2000, and 2005, and everything pointed to him meeting the same fate. Before the day was out, he had moved his entire government to the relative safety of the coastal city of Guayaquil – the conservative heartland of Ecuadorian merchant capital. That night, flanked by military generals, he delivered a televised address to the nation, in which he reaffirmed his commitment to the IMF reforms, and tried to play the old game of divide and rule, condemning the violence as the work of Venezuelan infiltrators and Correa stooges, while claiming common cause with the Indigenous social movements.[17] But the uprising continued unabated. The national transport network was now completely shut down. Events around the country on the 8th included the destruction of government buildings and the seizure of a hydroelectric dam. Meanwhile, the first marches began arriving in the capital. The Quito Hilton was trashed, and renegades breached security lines and surged into the National Assembly. Five hundred and seventy rebels were arrested on the 7th and the 8th, two were killed, and footage of extreme police violence began circulating on social media.[18]

Wednesday the 9th was a national strike, and Quito was a warzone. In a dramatic display of insurgent universality, the renegades on the front lines armed themselves with handmade shields, each of which was painted with an alternating message: "Popular Guard," "Indigenous Guard."[19] When battle commenced, they wielded whatever they could find. Cobblestones, paving slabs, drain covers, traffic bollards, and the steps of office buildings were all torn up and transformed into the ammunition of the people. The rebels attacked the presidential palace, but were forced back in thick clouds of teargas by heavily armed police firing rubber bullets and live rounds. Armored vehicles plunged into the crowds, flanked by cops on horseback and motorbike. The repression was more intense than ever, resulting in hundreds of injuries and three deaths.[20] Moreno had resisted the use of force throughout the *paro* in Dayuma, as a means of legitimizing his rule in contrast to the brutality of the Correa regime. But now he was unleashing bloodshed that far exceeded anything for which Correa had been responsible. When all else fails, unbridled state violence is the last resort against the insurgent universal.

Meanwhile, in the Amazon, the flow of oil that sustained the state was starting to run dry. The managers of CPP had seen this show more than once before. On the evening of Sunday, October 6, before the shit could hit the fan, they shut the *Obrador Central* in Dayuma and fled the Savage Road. The rest of the foreign oil companies quickly followed suit. They got out just in time. On Monday morning, stolen oil pipes were welded across the bridge in Dayuma, the bridge across the Napo, and the main bridge connecting Coca to the rest of the country. Barricades were erected in Inés Arango, and trees were felled in countless places up and down the *Vía Auca*. Soldiers approached the bridge in Dayuma but were warned off with blasts of dynamite. Smartphone footage shows two foolish cops trying to open another blockaded stretch of the road. They were disarmed and flung to the ground, before being chased back to their vehicle and body-slammed along the way. Block 61 was completely shut down. The same was the case for the Shushufindi field, where rebels seized control of the refinery. On the night of the 7th, insurgents stormed the central pumping station from which the oil of the Amazon is piped over the mountains to the coast, and managed to briefly shut it down. By the 9th, as Quito burned, national oil production had dropped by over 50 percent – from 500,000 barrels a day before the uprising, to just 244,000. For the first time since the ABP uprising of August 2005, the Ecuadorian government was forced to suspend oil exports.[21]

Reports of the state violence in Quito only served to further enrage the Amazonian insurgents. In the words of one *Kichwa* leader, "With the repression, it was as if the government was throwing gasoline on the people to make them catch alight."[22] A *Huaorani* community in the region of El Pindo had invited their *Shuar*, *Kichwa*, and mestizo neighbors to their annual fiesta. Everyone was in high spirits, when scenes of the repression seen on their mobile phones spurred them into action. They stormed the nearby camp of the detested oil company PetroOriental, expelling the security guards and stripping the place bare. They stole everything they could carry – televisions, laptops, pots and pans, tables, chairs, and beds. And anything they couldn't take they smashed with anarchic delight. In the words of one mestizo participant, it was the perfect combination of "rage of the *paro* and joy of the fiesta!"[23]

In Quito, the insurgents were equally outraged by the brutality of the police repression. And like their Amazonian comrades, they responded with the defiant staging of equality. On October 10, CONAIE paraded eight captured police officers in front of an audience of thousands in the cavernous auditorium of the House of Culture, which had been occupied by the uprising. The officers were forced to publicly apologize for the murders committed by their colleagues, and to carry a coffin symbolizing those who had lost their lives.[24] Over the following days, the battle in Quito continued to gather strength. Reinforcements arrived from across the country, including a militant contingent from the Savage Road, which was described as comprising "committed people, ready to kill and to die!"[25] Meanwhile, spontaneous forms of collective organization emerged to sustain the visiting fighters. Poor barrios across the city collected food and delivered it to makeshift kitchens in the park outside the House of Culture. Public universities opened their doors and were transformed into vast dormitories. Medical students tended to the wounded and invented homemade treatments to defend against the teargas. And all the while, on the frontlines, the battle raged. The demand of the *indígenas* was simple: not the isolated defense of a particular way of life, but the reinstatement of the fuel subsidy on which everyone's lives depended.

By October 12, the Ecuadorian government was on the brink of collapse. Oil production in the Amazon was continuing to diminish, as the army failed to break the multiple blockades. The battle on the bridge over the Napo was now so fierce that residents of nearby barrios had to abandon their houses to escape the teargas, which eventually ran out, forcing the soldiers to fling stones back at the barricades as they beat a fast retreat. Biker gangs patrolled the streets of Coca, shutting any open shops, and obliging their proprietors to join the uprising. When members of one gang were detained by the police, reinforcements swiftly arrived and detained the cops in turn. In the highlands, as in the Amazon, teargas supplies were running dry, and the renegades were rumored to be preparing to seize control of police stations and military bases. In Quito, food and water shortages were beginning to bite. The urban poor, the majority of whom had been supporting the *paro* from a safe distance, now assembled in their barrios and marched on the city center to join the battle on the streets. Government offices were sacked and burned to the ground, while those of the main television station were firebombed in retaliation for its false reporting.[26] Faced with the impending overthrow of the existing order, the rightwing press reported that the Quito elite had "furiously emerged" from their gated communities, "armed with golf clubs to defend their properties."[27]

With the state on its knees, Moreno finally agreed to enter negotiations with the CONIAE, which would be held the following evening, and broadcast on national television to ensure transparency. Meanwhile an unofficial truce fell into place across the country. Except, needless to say, in the region of the Savage Road. Pitched battles were still being fought on the streets of Coca, where soldiers chased insurgents deep into the barrios, firing fresh supplies of teargas into open doors and windows. Before long it was the soldiers themselves who were fleeing a lynching by the livid inhabitants. Reports of the torture of protesters in police custody led to the torching of a cop car and the capture of five policemen, who were tied to lampposts and doused in gasoline. But instead of burning them alive, the renegades abandoned them to their fate, and huddled around the doorways of any place with a TV that could be seen from the street. It was the eleventh night of an insurrection in which at least 11 of their comrades had been killed, with a further 1,340 injured and 1,192 arrested.[28] And now the negotiations were about to begin.

Moreno opened proceedings with a final patronizing appeal to ethnic difference, as a last-ditch attempt to divide the unity of the *paro*. He told the assembled *indígenas* that he knew they were good and honest people, and that they were not the ones committing violent acts, which were being orchestrated by malign external agents. If CONAIE would agree to call off the *paro*, then they could negotiate independently on matters related to their own particular Indigenous concerns. But Jaime Vargas ignored him. Instead, he thanked the people of Quito for their "unconditional solidarity" in support of the *paro*. "The request of the nation," he insisted, "is the revocation of Decree 883. If this is agreed at this moment, tranquility will immediately return to the entire country."[29]

The opening statements of the negotiations concluded with a speech by a *Kichwa* woman who had traveled from the Amazon: "The struggle is not only for the *indígenas*, but for the whole of Ecuador … mestizos, peasants, Afro-Ecuadorians, Indigenous *pueblos*, social sectors. We have all united with a single voice." Moreno had nothing to say in response. He slunk away into a backroom with his sidekicks, while the people waited with bated breath on the dark streets of Coca and across the nation. They needn't have worried. If he wanted to stay in power and prevent a revolution, the president of Ecuador simply had no choice. Two hours later the meeting reconvened, and the fuel subsidy was reinstated with immediate effect.

In the words of one of the rebels who had been straining to glimpse a TV from the rubble-strewn roadsides of Coca: "It was a profound feeling! It was an immense joy! Something incredible had happened. It was a victory against the government! Against the bourgeoisie! Against the IMF!"[30] At that moment, the bloody streets of Quito blossomed into an ardent carnival. Coca burned with fireworks and *aguardiente*. Motorbikes were kicked into gear. People piled into anything with wheels and an engine. And like a snake shedding its skin, the Savage Road shook off its barricades and became an incandescent caravan of struggle.

Notes

Chapter 1

1. Wilson, *Reality of Dreams*.
2. Thompson, *Fear and Loathing on the Campaign Trail*, 44; *Gonzo Papers*, 108.
3. Thompson's work in this regard includes studies of the Black Power and Chicano movements of the 1960s, and a portrait of the Hell's Angels when they were an illegal organization of marginalized renegades (Thompson, *Gonzo Papers* 39–47, 123–154; *Hell's Angels*).
4. Caron, "Hunter S. Thompson's 'Gonzo' Journalism"; Winston, *Gonzo Text*; Wright, "Literary, Political and Legal Strategies of Oscar Zeta Acosta and Hunter S. Thompson."
5. Bruce-Novoa, "Fear and Loathing," 40.
6. Thompson, *Fear and Loathing on the Campaign Trail*, 16–17 (emphasis added).
7. Thompson, *Happy Birthday, Jack Nicholson*, 24.
8. Danowski and Viveiros de Castro, *Ends of the World*; Escobar, "Beyond the Third World"; Grosfoguel, "Epistemic Decolonial Turn"; Mignolo, "Geopolitics of Sensing and Knowing"; Walsh, "'Other' Knowledges."
9. Danowski and Viveiros de Castro, *Ends of the World*, 56.
10. Dunlap and Jakobsen, *Violent Technologies of Extraction*, Gómez-Barris, *Extractive Zone*; Gudynas, "Extractivisms"; Riofrancos, *Resource Radicals*; Svampa, *Neo-Extractivism in Latin America*.
11. Escobar, *Designs for the Pluriverse*.
12. Kothari et al., "Introduction," xvii.
13. De la Cadena, "Indigenous Cosmopolitics," 360.
14. Walsh, "'Other' Knowledges," 15.
15. Buck-Morss, *Hegel*, 75.
16. Ibid.; James, *Black Jacobins*.
17. Linebaugh and Rediker, *Many-Headed Hydra* 4–6; 143–173.
18. Badiou, *Rebirth of History*, 79–80.
19. Buck-Morss, *Hegel*, 106.
20. Ibid., 133.
21. Tomba, *Insurgent Universality*, 41. Tomba's concept of insurgent universality captures the spirit of a broader reconceptualization and reaffirmation of universality in recent critical theory. See, for example, Badiou, *Saint Paul*; Dean, "Four Theses"; Haider, *Mistaken Identity*; Kapoor and Zalloua, *Universal Politics*; McGowan, *Universality and Identity Politics*; Wilson, "Insurgent Universal"; Žižek, *In Defense of Lost Causes*.
22. Žižek, *In Defense of Lost Causes*, 285.
23. Fanon, *Wretched of the Earth*, 236. Todd McGowan has developed this point as follows: "Fanon discusses the link between the colonized recognizing their participa-

tion in the universal and their struggle against colonialism. He states, 'At the very moment when they discover their humanity, they begin to sharpen their weapons to secure its victory.' Fanon's point here is that seeing themselves as universal – discovering their humanity – functions for the colonized as a weapon in the struggle against colonialism. Taking the side of those who don't belong to the colonial project places one on the side of the universal" (McGowan, *Universality and Identity Politics*, 76).

24. This potential oversight is evident, for example, in Catherine Walsh's methodological juxtaposition of "the hegemony, 'universality' and violence" of "Eurocentric modes of thinking" against "a different thought constructed and positioned from the histories and subjectivities of the people" (Walsh, "'Other' Knowledges," 12). This dichotomy would appear to leave little conceptual space for the possibility of a universality thought (or enacted) by "the people" themselves. The same can be said of Macarena Gómez-Barris's exploration of the social conflicts of the "extractive zone," which is framed by the question: "In zones of continual extractivism, what responses, engagements, and viewpoints emerge that do not exhaust difference but instead proliferate it?" (Gómez-Barris, *Extractive Zone*, xx). From such a starting point, eruptions of insurgent universality would seem destined to either be overlooked due to their apparent failure to "proliferate difference" or condemned for seemingly contributing to its "exhaustion."
25. Buck-Morss, *Hegel*, 151, 79. The critical literature on the political economy of extractivism includes a wide range of heterodox approaches in addition to those informed by decolonial theory (for an overview see Ye et al., "Incursions of Extractivism"). However, while this broader literature does not frame struggles over extractivism in terms of a pluriverse, neither does it explicitly consider their universal dimension, even when analyzing them in terms of class struggle (Veltmeyer, "Resistance"). Martin Arboleda's study of the Chilean mining industry is a significant exception in this regard, which argues that the universalizing drive of capital is not only destructive of cultural difference in its expansion of extractive frontiers, but also opens up the possibility for new forms of universal struggle to emerge across these differences (Arboleda, *Planetary Mine*).
26. Thompson, *Fear and Loathing in Las Vegas*, 80.
27. Ferrell and Hamm, *Ethnography at the Edge*.
28. Ferrell, "Criminological Verstehen," 30.
29. Badiou, *Rebirth of History*, 62. Beginning with Occupy Wall Street and the so-called Arab Spring, and recently sweeping through countries including France, Sudan, Lebanon, Iraq, Chile, Colombia, and Ecuador, before returning to the USA in the form of the Black Lives Matter protests of 2020, this wave of occupations and insurrections has been hailed by Badiou and others as heralding the rebirth of radical politics on a global scale. Like Badiou, Joshua Clover has drawn attention to the excessive, transcendent dimension of such events, which he frames in terms of a collective "surplus emotion … The moment when the partisans of riot exceed the police capacity for management, when the cops make their first retreat, is the moment when the riot becomes fully itself, slides loose from the grim continuity of daily life. The ceaseless social regulation that had seemed ideological and ambient and abstract is in this moment of surplus disclosed as a practical matter, open to social contest" (Clover, *Riot. Strike. Riot*, 1–2). For further analyses of our era of riots and uprisings, see, Bertho, *Age of Violence*; Bertelsen, "Effervescence"; Dikeç, *Urban Rage*; Dikeç and Swyngedouw, "Theorizing the Politicizing City"; Swyngedouw, *Promises of the Political*.
30. Badiou, *Greece*, 32.
31. Thompson, *Fear and Loathing on the Campaign Trail*, 48, 177. This book is an experiment in Thompson's methodology of edgework, to the extent that it is based primarily on my direct involvement in the uprising it depicts, which lasted for nine days from the morning of August 28, 2017, to the early hours of September 6. Prior

to the uprising, from 2014 to 2016, I spent two years living in Ecuador and conducting field research in the northern Amazon, much of which was focused on the oil industry, and which included visits to the *Vía Auca*. I had returned to the region to complete a different book based on this research (Wilson, *Reality of Dreams*), and already had a grasp of the complex social relations underlying the uprising, and personal contacts with a member of the local parish council and a Carmelite priest who contributed to the struggle. The description of events during the period of my own involvement is based on fieldnotes, photographs and audio recordings. I conducted further research on the uprising and its aftermath during two subsequent visits to the region – in 2018 and 2019, when I distributed articles that I had published about it in the Ecuadorian press to its participants. During these visits I sought and received the informed consent of the main protagonists for their inclusion in the book. Pseudonyms have been used for those communities whose members are implicated in what might be considered serious criminal acts. The communities in question are the *Shuar* community of "Kapáku" and the *Huaorani* community of "Obatawe." Both words mean "red" in their respective languages. Red is a symbolic color for both the *Shuar* and the *Huaorani* in times of struggle. It is also, of course, the color of international proletarian revolution. These pseudonyms thus refer to insurgent universality, in which the universal is embodied in particular identities, rather than erasing them beneath a homogenizing abstraction. The members of these communities have also been given pseudonyms. These are Spanish names, rather than *Shuar* or *Huaorani*, which is consistent with the actual names of these individuals. Some final details and clarifications were provided by interviews generously conducted by the anthropologist Natalia Valdivieso on my behalf in the region of the *Vía Auca* in March and April 2021. Throughout the text, all translations from Spanish are my own.

Chapter 2

1. Hecht and Cockburn, *Fate of the Forest*; Galarza, *El festín*; Watts, "Petro-Violence." Extractive frontiers such as the Ecuadorian Amazon constitute the cutting edge of global capitalism as a planetary system of endless accumulation, providing the materials demanded by its industrial centers and promising windfall profits to those with the power to plunder their resources. This frontier process forces open vast tracts of land, necessitating rapid infrastructural developments and triggering massive influxes of landless and workless populations, while encroaching on the territories of Indigenous peoples. All this occurs at the territorial and regulatory limits of the state, which is frequently present only in its most corrupt and repressive forms. Meanwhile, the resources themselves are spirited away to distant centers of production and consumption. These circumstances combine to shape the extractive frontier as a lawless space of ecological devastation, violent dispossession, and profound impoverishment, in which capital rules with impunity (Moore, *Capitalism*; Tsing, *Friction*; Watts, "Accumulating Insecurity.")
2. Cabodevilla, *La selva*; Lu et al., *Oil*; Martínez, *El Paraíso*.
3. Viteri, *Petróleo*, 147–176.
4. Oil worker, quoted in ibid., 193.
5. Ibid., 308.
6. Fontaine, *Los conflictos*.
7. Pichon, "Colonist Land Allocation"; Restrepo, "El proceso"; Sawyer, *Crude Chronicles*.
8. Valdivia, "Jugarse La Vida."
9. Schaefer, "Engaging Modernity."
10. An extensive literature exists on the impact of the oil industry in the Ecuadorian Amazon. See, for example, Cepek, *Life in Oil*; Lu et al., *Oil*; Rival, *Huaorani*

Transformations; Sawyer, *Crude Chronicles*. Very little, however, has been written about the colonization of the *Vía Auca*. Much of the historical detail in this chapter is accordingly drawn from author interviews with inhabitants of the region, conducted between 2015 and 2019.

11. Viteri, *Petróleo*, 314.
12. Fontaine, *Los conflictos*.
13. Pablo Gallegos, author interview, June 1, 2016, Coca, Ecuador. The population of the *Vía Auca* was approximately 8,000 in 2017, 21 percent of whom were Indigenous (Lu et al. *Oil*, 1). A survey of the entire northeast region of the Ecuadorian Amazon conducted in 1997 found that the vast majority of the migrant population came from the highlands and the coast. Over two-thirds of migrants were landless prior to their arrival, and most arrived in the Amazon with few if any assets. Only a quarter of migrants had completed primary school, and only 10 percent had continued in education beyond this preliminary level (Pichon, "Colonist Land Allocation.")
14. Viteri, *Petróleo*, 322–351.
15. Cabodevilla, *Zona intangible*; Pichon, "Colonist Land Allocation"; Wesche, "Ecotourism."
16. Kimerling, *Amazon Crude*; Larrea, "Extractivism"; Pichon, "Colonist Land Allocation."
17. Cepek, "Loss of Oil", 395.
18. Parishes of South Orellana, "Informe de inspecciones a zonas contaminadas por la actividad hodrocarburificas (sic) en el Campo Auca", January 27, 2006. This report was submitted by the parish councils of the *Via Auca*, in their campaign for compensation and environmental remediation from the state oil company, Petroecuador. The report is a compilation of inspections conducted between February 2005 and January 2006 but is indicative of the situation that had persisted in the region since the early 1990s.
19. Gonzalo Plazarte, author interview, August 21, 2018, Dayuma, Ecuador.
20. MPD Sucumbíos, *Las valerosas jornadas*; Wilson, *Reality of Dreams*, 53–62.
21. Gonzalo Plazarte, author interview, August 21, 2018, Dayuma.
22. Dositeo Cuenca, community leader and activist, author interview, September 2, 2018, Dayuma.
23. Here, and throughout the book, my accounts of such events are based on interviews and conversations with local militants, politicians, activists, and community members.
24. MPD Sucumbíos, *Las Valerosas Jornadas*; Ortiz, "Protestas"; "Sigcha, Sucumbíos y Orellana."
25. Jhon Rosero, author interview, August 31, 2018, Dayuma.
26. Correa's speech can be seen at "Cadena Radial Nro. 74 desde Lago Agrio, Sucumbíos": https://www.youtube.com/watch?v=_yknetMTiNo (accessed September 26, 2017).
27. Humberto Piajuaje, activist and member of the ABP, author interview, June 14, 2015, Lago Agrio, Ecuador.
28. Provincial Government of Orellana, "Acta de la asamblea de la provincial de Orellana, 13 de enero de 2007" (personal archives of Enrique Morales, one of the leading figures in the ABP.)
29. The implementation of this experiment in the Ecuadorian Amazon is explored in Wilson, *Reality of Dreams*.
30. Enrique Morales, author interview, August 22, 2017, Coca.
31. Legal Team of PetroOriental, "Relación circunstanciada de los hechos," submitted to the public prosecutor of Orellana, who submitted it in turn to the chief of police of Orellana, as part of *Oficio No. 1320-2007-MFDSYO-FO*, July 5, 2007 (personal archives of Enrique Morales).
32. Jhon Rosero, author interview, August 24, 2016, Dayuma.

33. The information in this section is drawn from interviews and discussions with Guadalupe Llori and other participants in the events described, as well as a report on a visit by a ministerial delegation conducted in the aftermath of the conflict (Cuenca, "Informe.")
34. Llori, "Carta abierta."
35. Correa's speech can be seen in "Cadena Radial 25 07/07/2007" available at https://www.youtube.com/watch?v=K1yP6dXnqjM (accessed July 18, 2019).
36. Letter reproduced in Aguirre, *Dayuma*, 124. Tensions in the region had further intensified in October 2007, when the community of La Cristalina launched a small *paro*, shutting down a single oil well in the region of Tiguino, at the far end of the Savage Road, to demand the clean-up of an oil spill. The private security of the Belorussian company Petrobell intervened with the support of the Ecuadorian military. A confrontation ensued in which one of the community members, Segundo López, was killed (Aguirre, *Dayuma*, 77).
37. Ibid., 24.
38. Chief of Police of Orellana, "Informando del paro en la parroquia de Dayuma" *Oficio 2373* December 2, 2007 (reproduced in Aguirre, *Dayuma*, 106–109). Unless otherwise indicated, the following chronology of the *paro* – including direct quotations – is based on the contents of this report. The claims made in such reports are often questionable at best. However, the majority of the incidents that the report describes regarding the actions of the militants have been confirmed in interviews with those involved in the events themselves.
39. Chief of Security for the Auca oilfield, "*Paro* en la parroquia de Dayuma" *Memorando No.23-Seg-Auca-2007*, November 26, 2007 (reproduced in Aguirre, *Dayuma*, 103–105).
40. Ibid.
41. Quoted in ibid., 57.
42. "Informando del paro en la parroquia de Dayuma," internal police report, Orellana branch, December 2, 2007, (reproduced in Aguirre, *Dayuma*, 109).
43. Correa's speech can be heard in the second part of the documentary *Dayuma Nunca Mas!* Available at: https://www.youtube.com/watch?v=jUN-gcjvxT0 (accessed July 18, 2019).
44. Jhon Rosero, author interview, August 31, 2018, Dayuma.

Chapter 3

1. Enrique Morales, author interview, August 22, 2017, Coca.
2. Becker, "Ecuador"; Becker and Riofrancos, "Souring Friendship"; Ospina, "Orden de prisión."
3. Enrique Morales, author interview, August 22, 2017, Coca.
4. *El Comercio*, "Auca"; Petroamazonas, "Informe técnico." Block 61 occupies 78,300 hectares of jungle along both sides of the *Vía Auca*, and overlaps the parishes of El Dorado, Taracoa, Dayuma, and Inés Arango. It includes the main field of Auca Central and the satellite fields of Yuca, Yulebra, Culebra, Anaconda, Pitalala, Boa, Anura, Auca Sur, Auca Este, Conga, Conga Sur, Cononaco, Rumiyacu, Chonta Este, and Chonta Sur.
5. *El Universo*, "Auca."
6. Purcell and Martínez, "Post-neoliberal energy modernity."
7. *El Comercio*, "Ecuador"; "La petrolera estatal."
8. Petroamazonas was created in 2007, when it assumed control of the majority of state oil production, with Petroecuador focused primarily on the commercial side of the industry.

9. Fun-Sang et al., "Restoring"; Petroamazonas, "Informe técnico"; Villavicencio, "Otra más."
10. *El Telégrafo*, "Bloque 61"; Fun-Sang, "Restoring."
11. *La Hora*, "Campo Auca."
12. Jose Icaza Romero, quoted in *El Telégrafo*, "Bloque 61."
13. *El Comercio*, "Auca"; "La petrolera estatal"; Villavicencio, "Exclusivo"; "Otra más."
14. Villavicencio, "Otra más."
15. Santos, "El entreguismo."
16. Villavicencio, "Exclusivo."
17. Fernando Santos, quoted in *Ecuavisa*, "Conozca."
18. Wilson and Bayón, *Selva de los elefantes blancos*.
19. *Financial Times*, "Schlumberger." The case of Schlumberger epitomizes the intimate relationship between financialization and labor exploitation in the oil industry. As Mazen Labban has demonstrated, while companies like Schlumberger are increasingly focused on boosting their stock prices through the maximization of shareholder value in the sphere of finance, this is ultimately achieved in large part through layoffs, wage cuts, worsening working conditions, and union suppression in the sphere of production (Labban, "Against Shareholder Value").
20. According to the journalist who revealed the background to the contract for Block 61, "Schlumberger's economic model forgot to account for the fact that the entire production of the Auca field until 2024 had already been committed to the payment of Chinese debt … In other words, there was no oil to pay Schlumberger" (Villavicencio, "Otra más.") The oil produced in Block 61 had not been specifically earmarked for this purpose. But in December 2017, the Ecuadorian government revealed that 100 percent of Ecuadorian oil exports in 2018 would be used to pay down Chinese debt. This percentage would gradually diminish over time, amounting to an estimated 20 percent of oil exports in 2024 (*El Comercio*, "El 100%.") Given that Block 61 represented 19 percent of national production at the time, a quantity of oil equivalent to the entire production of the block would be devoted to this cause during this period.
21. *Argus*, "Schlumberger."
22. Techint, *Techint Group*, 57, 42.
23. This was Jhon Rosero's understanding of the situation. There were several competing accounts of the chicanery – legal or otherwise – through which the payment of *utilidades* was avoided in this case, including perspectives offered to me by a labor lawyer and an academic specialist in the field. Of all these accounts, Rosero's explanation was the most widely propounded and the most convincing. What is certain is that Schlumberger was desperate to reduce costs in any way possible. In the same month that CGA was established, Schlumberger reported a loss of $1.56 per share for the second quarter of 2016 and announced another 8,000 layoffs (*Oil Price*, "The Worst"). Two months previously, the CEO of Schlumberger had warned that "the exploration and production industry finds itself in the deepest financial crisis on record" (*Rig Zone*, "Schlumberger"). Beyond these limited facts in the public domain, the opacity of the business operations of the company and its affiliates in Block 61 – demonstrated by the lack of clarity regarding its avoidance of paying *utilidades* – is illustrative of the power of capital over labor in the multinational oil industry.
24. *Business Insider*, "Schlumberger."
25. The information in this section is drawn from interviews with those involved in the events, as well as an eyewitness report by a public notary conducted on request of CGA on August 24, 2017; a Private Security Report submitted to CGA by Jara Seguridad – a security company – on August 31, 2017; and a statement about these events submitted by the legal team of CGA to the Labor Ministry on September 4, 2017.
26. All direct quotes from the *paro* were recorded at the scene, apart from some short phrases, which were scribbled down at times when the recorder was switched off.

Chapter 4

1. The kidnapping of Esteban García was recounted in great detail by many of those involved. Their testimonies were corroborated by a meticulous internal report on the event prepared by the private security company hired by CGA in Block 61, which was passed on to me by one of the members of the *comité*. The report includes a minute-by-minute breakdown of the act, beginning at 13:54 with the storming of the *Obrador Central* by the *Shuar* (several of whom are identified by name), and concluding at 13:57 with the hijacking of the Petroamazonas truck.
2. Informal conversation with a member of staff at the Hotel Auca, September 10, 2017, Coca.
3. The bureaucrat is faithfully reproducing the fictitious version of events included in the police report on the arrests of Luis Barberan and Jimmy Chamba (aka Tilapia), who were accused of blocking a fuel tanker and charged with "Paralyzation of the Distribution of Gasoline" under Article 262 of the Integral Penal Code, which became law in 2014. This law made "the obstruction of a public service" a criminal offence. Furthermore, this offence could be prosecuted not only as a minor crime but as a form of "sabotage and terrorism." Whereas previously it had been difficult to prosecute those involved in *paros*, now any company or institution could wield the charge of sabotage and terrorism against those it considered to be impeding its activities, particularly when operating in tandem with a corrupt and servile police force and judiciary, as in this case.
4. Many would argue that the provocation of an incident that can justify a violent intervention is precisely the army's intention in such situations. In the words of a human rights activist based in Coca: "The military never arrive in a pacifistic manner. They are always looking for ways to anger the civilian population. And as there are a lot of people [at a *paro*], and they have often been there for days with little sleep, and they haven't been eating properly, and their nerves are in shreds (*están con los nervios a punta*), they can easily lose control and at that moment the army can blame the community and say: 'We had to act to protect the peace.' But it is the company that calls upon them to repress the people" (Diocles Zambrano, author interview, August 29, 2018, Coca).
5. The fear engendered by the spears amongst those whose interests the police are representing is evident from a letter sent be CGA's legal team to the public prosecutor of Orellana on October 26, during the sit-down strike prior to the uprising: "We request that the National Police, in coordination with the Armed Forces ... proceed to remove the people currently located in different worksites throughout Block 61 .. in the name of civilian peace and respect for the property of others, avoiding the continuation of the [current] state of terror in the region, [which involves] acts that endanger the lives and the physical integrity of the population, given that they are threatening to launch attacks with the wooden spears that they have in their control." As this passage also reveals, CGA's management were explicitly calling for military intervention prior to uprising, and these calls must surely have intensified in the context of the *paro*.

Chapter 5

1. Seeing *sapos* everywhere could be considered a consequence of this burgeoning paranoia. But the crucial role of such informants in providing inside information on the *paro* is demonstrated by internal company documents with which I was later provided. These include detailed daily reports on the *paro* supplied by *sapos* operating within it.
2. Chimbo and Charango were running against Manuel Méndez and Darío Rodríguez, who had created the *comité*, whereas Chimbo and Charango had played no part in its foundation. According to Méndez, the aim of CGA in backing these two candidates

was to depoliticize the *comité* and ensure its collaboration with the management. Charango was known to have played a similar role in the past, as part of the corrupt official union of the state oil company Petroecuador. The workers easily saw through this strategy, and Darío and Méndez won the election by 400 votes to 70. Since then, Chimbo and Charango had been their sworn enemies.

3. Coca Visión, "Continua la medida de resistencia de los trabajadores de la empresa CGA" September 1, 2017.
4. Cabodevilla, "Ecuador Estratégico."
5. The translation of these lyrics from *Shuar* to Spanish was provided by a member of the Kapáku community. The subsequent translation from Spanish to English is my own.
6. Diocles Zambrano, Centro de Derechos Humanos de Orellana, author interview, August 24, 2017, Coca.
7. Black and red are the principal colors used in *Shuar* face and body paint. Whereas red is associated with positivity and attraction, black is associated with negativity and repulsion, and is worn to guard against vengeful spirits (Chacón Zhapán et al., *Sabiduría de la Cultura Shuar*, 46). Given the recently discovered murder plot, it is therefore unsurprising that the red of *achiote* was replaced by the black of charcoal on the bodies of many *Shuar* men on this day, when they were due to confront their mortal enemies. Although I was told that black was being worn to represent oil, it seems likely that this deeper meaning was entangled with the symbolization of petroleum. Ethnographers working with *Shuar* communities in the Ecuadorian and Peruvian Amazon have noted the increasing prevalence of such entanglements, which has been explained as a consequence of intensified engagement with mestizo culture and extractive capital (Mader, *Metamorfosis del poder*).
8. According to *Shuar* mythology, a *Shuar* man named Jempe transformed himself into a hummingbird, and flew to the house of Takéa, the sole possessor of fire, who would kill anyone who tried to acquire it. Jempe arrived at Takéa's house on a stormy night, bedraggled and shivering, and was placed beside the fire to recover. As soon as his wings were dry, he ignited them in the flames, and flitted out of the door before Takéa could shut it. He then flew through the jungle, setting fire to the trees with his burning wings, and thus bringing fire to the *Shuar* (Pellizaro, *Mitologia Shuar*, 5–15).

Chapter 6

1. Internal security brief produced by Jara Seguridad (the private security company employed by CGA), covering October 5–9, 2017. This document and several others drawn on in this chapter were included in a set of private security briefs and legal letters submitted by CGA as part of a legal case against one of the leaders of the *paro*, who provided me with a copy of the material. The documents include extensive security camera footage and precise minute-by-minute breakdowns of key events in the first few days of the second *paro*. The information presented in this chapter also draws on TV clips and mobile phone footage posted on YouTube, and the archives of a local cable news station that produced several reports on the events that unfolded in Dayuma and along the *Vía Auca* after my departure, which were generously shared with me by the journalists and editors involved. (Some of the references in this regard have been withheld to protect the anonymity of certain protagonists.) Apart from these sources, the chapter is primarily based on interviews conducted in August and September 2018 with key actors involved in the events described, and fieldnotes taken during my travels up and down the Savage Road.
2. Rivas, "Schlumberger."
3. "Población de Dayuma decidió seguir con la medida de resistencia – Teleamazonas" https://www.youtube.com/watch?v=ACYuPpQrXXM (accessed July 25, 2019).

This was the first and only time that a national news network reported on the *paro*. (Although Teleamazonas had been present for the negotiations on October 5, that report was never broadcast, perhaps because the story of a successful proletarian mestizo–Indigenous struggle was unappealing to Ecuadorian elites.) Unfortunately – though unsurprisingly – the report that I cite here is incoherent and misleading, and contains multiple inaccuracies. For example, a *Huaorani* leader is misidentified as a *Kichwa* leader, and an opponent of the *comité* is misidentified as their spokesperson.

4. Member of the parish council of Dayuma, author interview, August 17, 2018, Dayuma.
5. "Conaie y Confeniae respaldan paralización en Dayuma 19-10-17 Radio Musical" https://www.youtube.com/watch?v=6qFtbX5vWKs (accessed July 25, 2019).
6. Diocles Zambrano, author interview, August 29, 2018, Coca.
7. Inés Arango is the most isolated and impoverished of the four parishes of Block 61. At the time of the *paro*, the houses in the center of the parish capital of Western – named after a foreign oil company that had once operated in the area – only had running water for four hours a day, while the rest had none at all. The electricity supply in the parish was limited to *fincas* located directly alongside the *Vía Auca*, most of the local stretch of which remained unpaved.
8. Edison Kapáku, author interview, August 29, 2018, Coca.
9. According to Enrique Morales, this figure was quoted by a representative of Petroamazonas during a subsequent meeting at which he was present. The figure included revenues lost due to the closure of wells, and the delay in the opening of new wells caused by the paralyzation of CGA. (Author interview, August 13, 2018, Coca.)
10. Edison Kapáku, author interview, August 29, 2018, Coca.
11. Darío Rodríguez, author interview, August 14, 2018, Coca.
12. A photocopy of the agreement was provided to me by Darío Rodríguez. Strictly speaking, the fine in question was issued to Shaya, the subsidiary through which Schlumberger operates in Block 61. According to Enrique Morales, the fine was indeed issued, and was the highest fine that could legally be applied although this only amounted to $20,000 or so, which is of course insignificant compared to the multibillion dollar contract itself. (Author interview, August 13, 2018, Coca).
13. "Retorna la paz a Dayuma 25-10-17 Radio Musical" https://www.youtube.com/watch?v=XFGfrozf8LE (accessed July 25, 2019).
14. Coca Visión, "Informe: paro en Dayuma", October 27, 2017. The worker's name was Simon Bolívar Balzeca. Mobile phone footage of his body on the road was shown to me by a fellow participant in the *paro*. Another of his comrades recalled the situation as follows: "And as a result of [the betrayal of the agreement and the resumption of the *paro*] a *compañero* left for his house, very resentful and disillusioned, and that led to his death … He said 'I have to maintain my children … I have to go, because I really have to work and there is no solution to this situation' … And he left. And leaving in that way, a kilometer or so from Dayuma he had an accident … Later we went to visit his family, and yes, it was a very poor family, with many necessities" (Klever Loor, author interview, September 4, 2018, Coca).
15. Nasdaq, "Schlumberger's operations"; Reuters, "Ecuador to sign payment."
16. The WhatsApp conversations discovered on the smartphone of Esteban García, the operations manager of CGA, had revealed that in the initial phase of the *paro*, CGA was refusing to negotiate with the *comité* on the explicit instruction of Schlumberger. It is therefore highly probable that CPP was also acting on Schlumberger's instruction in this case.
17. Coca Visión, "Paro en Dayuma continua," November 16, 2017; Coca Visión, "Paro en Dayuma: reacciones por presos," November 17, 2017; Menardo Shinge, president of Taracoa, author interview, August 28, 2018, Coca.
18. Edison Kapáku, author interview, August 29, 2018, Coca; Marco Kapáku, author interview, August 23, 2018, Coca.

19. Employee dispossessed and reinstated by CGA, author interview, August 30, 2017, Rumbipamba, Ecuador; Guillermo Grefa, ex-president of Rumbipamba, author interview, August 31, 2018, Rumbipamba.
20. Coca Visión, "El Dorado levanta medida de resistencia por acuerdo firmado entre desempleados y Petroamazonas," February 8, 2018; Coca Visión, "Nacionalidades y desempleados anuncian paro viernes 8 de marzo por las calles de la ciudad," February 28, 2018; Luis Etza, historical *Shuar* leader in El Pindo, and one of the organizers of the demonstration demanding the dismissal of the governor, author interview, August 24, 2018, Coca.
21. In 2003, members of the *Huaorani* led a massacre of *Taromenane* on behalf of illegal loggers. A further massacre of *Taromenane* by *Huaorani* took place in 2013 (Lu et al., *Oil*: 329–235, 244–252).
22. This is reported in an internal memorandum of the Ministry of Hydrocarbons, which details a visit to Obatawe in September 2016.
23. The public prosecutor had demanded that Esteban García's smartphone be submitted as evidence. According to Darío Rodríguez, as soon as the incriminating evidence had been secured, the public prosecutor ceased to pursue the case. The managers then launched a counter case against Marco Kapáku and himself for harassment (*maliciosa y temeraria*), which they were now defending themselves against. (Author interview, August 14, 2018, Coca).
24. Commenting on the firing of the representatives of the *comité*, Jhon Rosero noted: "The money of the oil company has divided the people from their leaders. The people have to decide between supporting their leader or defending their job … There have been many good leaders, who have fought heart and soul in the struggles, but have ended up betrayed by their own people. That is the most serious consequence of everything that has happened here." (Author interview, August 31, 2018, Dayuma).
25. Outreach worker, author interview, September 8, 2018, Quito.
26. Diocles Zambrano, author interview, August 29, 2018, Coca.
27. Guillermo Grefa, author interview, August 31, 2018, Rumbipamba.
28. The sale of jobs was one of the most persistent rumors, and it was not only Judith Hidalgo who was said to be involved. All three other parish council presidents were also accused by some and absolved by others, as were the presidents of various Indigenous communities. In order to comply with Ecuadorian law, oil companies are obliged to hire 80 percent of unskilled labor locally. Parish council presidents were accused of accepting payment in exchange for registering workers from other places as residents of their parish, and assisting them in securing the available jobs. In the case of the presidents of Indigenous communities, the guarantee of jobs for the community, acquired through *paros*, would allegedly allow unscrupulous presidents to sell these jobs to people from outside the community, behind the backs of their fellow *comuneros*.
29. It should also be noted that the estimated $31 million of *utilidades* owed to the workers for 2016–2017 were never paid. (This was pointed out to me by Klever Loor, one of the CGA employees fired and charged with sabotage and terrorism for his role in the wildcat strike of April 2017, author interview, September 4, 2018, Coca.)
30. Blum, "Schlumberger rebounding."

Chapter 7

1. Buck-Morss, "Gift of the Past," 181.
2. Bakhtin, *Rabelais and His World*, 10, 9. Bakhtin's account of medieval carnival has been interpreted as a coded celebration of the radical potentialities of the Russian Revolution, and a ciphered critique of its betrayal by the Stalinist order under which

he lived (Holquist, "Prologue"). Tomba has identified this early phase of the Russian Revolution as an instance of insurgent universality (Tomba, *Insurgent Universality*, 120–185).

3. Badiou, *Rebirth of History*, 94.
4. Buck-Morss, "Commonist," 67.
5. Buck-Morss, *Hegel*, ix.
6. Mignolo, "Geopolitics of Knowledge," 70; "Geopolitics of Sensing and Knowing," 280.
7. Tomba, *Insurgent Universality*, 19.
8. Rivera Cusicanqui, "Ch'ixinakax Utxiwa," 102, 104. A similar argument has been made by David Graeber in his response to a critique of his work by the decolonial scholar Eduardo Viveiros de Castro, who accuses Graeber of dogmatically projecting Marxist categories onto the Indigenous subjects of his research, despite the fact that Graeber explicitly challenges orthodox Marxism on the basis of his ethnographic material. "Presumably, then," Graeber suggests, "Viveiros de Castro's objection is not that I fail to use the ethnographic material to problematize my theoretical assumptions, but rather that I fail to do so in the way he believes I should." Like my interpretation of events on the Savage Road as an instance of insurgent universality, which rejects Eurocentric universalism from a perspective very different to that of mainstream decolonial theory, Graeber insists that Indigenous peoples should not be confined within their respective corners of the pluriverse, but "can teach us something unexpected about humans everywhere." From this perspective, as Graeber concludes, it is the disavowed cultural relativism of decolonial orthodoxy that "places people in boxes not of their own devising" (Graeber, "Radical Alterity," 5, 6, 34).
9. Haider, *Mistaken Identity*, 37.
10. Ibid., 113 (emphasis in original). The defeat of the uprising on the Savage Road is only a relatively minor recent example in the history of state strategies of racial and ethnic division, which is as long as the history of capitalism itself. For example, Linebaugh and Rediker have detailed the ways in which the motley crew that formed aboard the pirate ships of the seventeenth century was eventually fragmented by racial separations (Linebaugh and Rediker, *Many-Headed Hydra*, 333–334); Buck-Morss has noted how the universality of the Haitian revolution was replaced by the ethnonationalism of the Haitian state (Buck-Moss, *Hegel*, 146–147); and Haider has demonstrated that the divisive racial categories that underpinned Black slavery in the USA were originally designed to undermine a collective movement of Black and white proletarians against the colonial planter class (Haider, *Mistaken Identity*, 51–58).
11. Dean, "Four Theses."
12. Žižek, *Ticklish Subject* 201, emphasis in original. Building on this point, Ilan Kapoor and Zahi Zalloua note that a universality grounded not in a common essence but in a shared antagonism "is (and can only be) taken up from a particular vantage point. It is always partial, partisan, engaged. One's response to the antagonism of one's position never happens neutrally or objectively: it unfolds only by taking sides." Drawing on Fanon's critique of any anti-colonial politics that bases itself on "mummified tradition," they argue that in contrast to such fetishization of cultural difference, a radical universality grounded in an excluded particularity "is never predefined or given; it is always struggled for, incomplete, and in the making" (Kapoor and Zalloua 2021: 18–19, quoting Fanon). This is the universality that emerged on the Savage Road through a collective identification with a particular identity, which was evoked in the claim that "We are all Indigenous!" and actualized by taking the same side in an antagonistic struggle against state and capital.
13. Buck-Morss, "Gift of the Past," 183.
14. Jose Miguel Goldáraz, author interview, November 25, 2019, Coca. In November 2019, I traveled to Ecuador to learn about the events of the preceding month, and to

distribute copies of a further article I had published about the *paro* to its main protagonists. The following account draws on interviews conducted in Quito, Coca, and Dayuma, as well as informal conversations and my own observations.

15. Collyns, "Ecuador moves"; "Ecuador paralyzed"; Santillana, "Protestas."
16. Collyns, "Ecuador moves"; *El Comercio*, "CONAIE y FUT"; *El Comercio*, "Manifestaciones."
17. CNN, "Lenín Moreno traslada sede del Gobierno de Ecuador a Guayaquil", available at: https://www.youtube.com/watch?v=7duflXNIH_g (accessed April 4, 2020).
18. *Associated Press*, "Indigenous protestors"; *El Comercio*, "Las instalaciones."
19. *El Comercio*, "Defensoría."
20. Collyns, "Ecuador paralyzed"; "Ecuador: defiant protesters."
21. *El Comercio*, "Petroecuador"; *Primacias*, "Paro afecta."
22. Guillermo Grefa, author interview, November 27, 2019, Dayuma.
23. Inhabitant of El Dorado, author interview, November 22, 2019, Coca.
24. Collyns, "Ecuador: defiant protesters."
25. Guillermo Grefa, author interview, November 27, 2019, Dayuma.
26. *Associated Press*, "Army deployed."
27. *El Comercio*, "91 vías cerradas."
28. Santillana, "Protestas."
29. *Telesur*, "Líderes indígenas y pdte. ecuatoriano debaten sobre el decreto 883": https://www.youtube.com/watch?v=6XMDbe5D5RM (accessed April 4, 2020).
30. Participant in the 2019 uprising, author interview, November 19, 2019, Coca.

References

Aguirre, Milagros. *Dayuma ¡Nunca Mas!* Quito: CICAME, 2008.

Arboleda, Martín. *Planetary Mine: Territories of Extraction under Late Capitalism.* New York: Verso, 2020.

Argus. "Schlumberger presses to collect Ecuador oil fees" March 24, 2017: https://oglinks.news/schlumberger/news/presses-to-collect-ecuador-oil-fees (accessed July 15, 2019).

Associated Press. "Indigenous protesters converge on Quito as Ecuador president moves out" reproduced in *The Guardian*, October 8, 2019: https://www.theguardian.com/world/2019/oct/08/protesters-swarm-ecuador-capital-as-president-moves-out (accessed April 4, 2020).

Associated Press. "Army deployed in Ecuador as protests descend into violence" reproduced in *The Guardian*, October 13, 2019: https://www.theguardian.com/world/2019/oct/13/army-deployed-in-ecuador-as-protests-descend-into-violence (accessed April 4, 2020).

Badiou, Alain. *Saint Paul: The Foundation of Universalism*. Stanford: Stanford University Press, 2003.

Badiou, Alain. *The Rebirth of History: Times of Riots and Uprisings*. London: Verso, 2012.

Badiou, Alain. *Greece and the Reinvention of Politics*. London: Verso, 2018.

Bakhtin, Mikhail. *Rabelais and His World*. Bloomington: Indiana University Press, 1984.

Becker, Marc. "Ecuador: Slowing a conservative restoration" *NACLA Report on the Americas* 49:2 (2017) 127–131.

Becker, Marc and Thea N. Riofrancos. "A souring friendship, a left divided" *NACLA Report on the Americas* 50:2 (2018) 124–127.

Bertelsen, Bjørn Enge. "Effervescence and ephemerality: Popular urban uprisings in Mozambique" *Ethnos* 81:1 (2016) 25–52.

Bertho, Alain. *The Age of Violence: The Crisis of Political Action and the End of Utopia*. London: Verso, 2018.

Blum, Jordan. "Schlumberger rebounding after cutting 70,000 jobs" *Chron.com*, March 6, 2018: https://www.chron.com/business/energy/article/Schlumberger-rebounding-after-cutting-70-000-jobs-12731802.php (accessed November 21, 2019).

Bruce-Novoa. "Fear and loathing on the buffalo trail" *MELUS* 6:4 (1979) 39–50.

Buck-Morss, Susan. *Hegel, Haiti, and Universal History*. Pittsburgh: University of Pittsburgh Press, 2009.

Buck-Morss, Susan. "The gift of the past" *Small Axe* 14:3 (2010) 173–185.

Buck-Morss, Susan. "A commonist ethics" in *The Idea of Communism 2*, edited by Slavoj Žižek (57–76). New York: Verso, 2013.

Business Insider. "Schlumberger: Rising costs hurt margins" April 21, 2017: https://www.businessinsider.com/schlumberger-earnings-q1-2017-2017-4?r=US&IR=T (accessed July 15, 2019).

Cabodevilla, Miguel Ángel. *La selva de los fantasmas errantes*. Pompeya: CICAME, 1997.

Cabodevilla, Miguel Ángel. *Zona Intangible ¡Peligro de muerte!* Quito: CICAME, 2008.

Cabodevilla, Miguel Ángel. "Ecuador Estratégico y los hechos aislados" *La Linea de Fuego*, April 18, 2014: https://lalineadefuego.info/2014/04/18/ecuador-estrategico-y-los-hechos-aislados-por-miguel-angel-cabodevilla/ (accessed July 10, 2020).

Caron, James E. "Hunter S. Thompson's "Gonzo" journalism and the tall tale tradition in America" *Studies in Popular Culture* 8:1 (1985) 1–16.

Cepek, Michael. "The loss of oil: Constituting disaster in Amazonian Ecuador" *The Journal of Latin American and Caribbean Anthropology* 17:3 (2012) 393–412.

Cepek, Michael. *Life in Oil: Cofán Survival in the Petroleum Fields of Amazonia*. Austin: University of Texas Press, 2018.

Chacón Zhapán, Juan, et al. *Sabiduría de la Cultura Shuar de la Amazonía Ecuatoriana Tomo II*. Cuenca: Universidad de Cuenca, 2012.

Clover, Joshua. *Riot. Strike. Riot: The New Era of Uprisings*. London: Verso, 2019.

Collyns, Dan. "Ecuador moves government out of capital as violent protests rage" *The Guardian*, October 8, 2019: https://www.theguardian.com/world/2019/oct/08/ecuador-moves-government-out-of-capital-as-violent-protests-rage (accessed April 4, 2020).

Collyns, Dan. "Ecuador paralyzed by national strike as Moreno refuses to step down" *The Guardian*, October 9, 2019: https://www.theguardian.com/world/2019/oct/09/ecuador-strike-lenin-moreno-latest (accessed April 4, 2020.)

Collyns, Dan. "Ecuador: defiant protesters parade captured officers as unrest drags on" *The Guardian*, October 10, 2019: https://www.theguardian.com/world/2019/oct/10/ecuador-indigenous-protesters-parade-captured-officers (accessed April 4, 2020).

Cuenca, Dositeo. *Informe de la inspección con las autoridades del ministerio de gobernó en la parroquia Dayuma cantón y provincia de Orellana*. Dayuma: Asociación de campesinos Rodrigo Borja, 2007 (personal archives of Dositeo Cuenca).

Danowski, Déborah and Eduardo Viveiros de Castro. *The Ends of the World*. Cambridge: Polity, 2017.

De la Cadena, Marisol. "Indigenous cosmopolitics in the Andes: Conceptual reflections beyond 'politics'" *Cultural Anthropology* 25:2 (2010) 334–370.

Dean, Jodi. "Four theses on the comrade" *E-Flux Journal* 86 (2017) 1–16.

Dikeç, Mustafa. *Urban Rage: The Revolt of the Excluded*. New Haven: Yale University Press, 2017.

Dikeç, Mustafa and Erik Swyngedouw. "Theorizing the politicizing city" *International Journal of Urban and Regional Research* 41:1 (2017) 1–18.

Dunlap, Alexander and Jostein Jakobsen. *The Violent Technologies of Extraction: Political Ecology, Critical Agrarian Studies, and the Capitalist Worldeater*. New York: Palgrave Macmillan, 2020.

Ecuavisa. "Conozca que se negoció en el campo petrolero Auca-Bloque 61" December 15, 2015: https://www.ecuavisa.com/articulo/noticias/actualidad/124369-conozca-que-se-negocio-campo-petrolero-auca-bloque-61 (accessed July 15, 2019).

El Comercio. "Auca, una de las áreas petroleras más productivas" December 16, 2015: https://www.elcomercio.com/actualidad/petrolera-petroamazonas-firmo-convenio-schlumberger.html (accessed December 15, 2018).

El Comercio. "La petrolera estatal firmó un convenio por USD 4,900 millones de Schlumberger" December 16, 2015: https://www.elcomercio.com/actualidad/petrolera-petroamazonas-firmo-convenio-schlumberger.html (accessed December 15, 2018).

El Comercio. "Ecuador recibió USD 18,170 millones en anticipos petroleros y prestamos" February 21, 2017: https://www.elcomercio.com/actualidad/ecuador-anticipospetroleros-prestamos.html (accessed July 15, 2019).

El Comercio. "El 100% del crudo exportable del 2018 está comprometido" December 17, 2017: https://www.elcomercio.com/actualidad/petroleo-exportable-comprometido-negocios-hidrocarburos.html (accessed July 15, 2019).

El Comercio. "CONAIE y FUT dicen que 20,000 indígenas llegarán a Quito y condicionan diálogo con el Gobierno" October 7, 2019: https://www.elcomercio.com/actualidad/conaie-fut-indigenas-quito-dialogo.html (accessed April 4, 2020).

El Comercio. "Manifestaciones continuaron con saqueos y cierres viales" October 8, 2019: https://www.elcomercio.com/actualidad/manifestaciones-saqueos-cierres-viales-indigenas.html (accessed April 4, 2020).

El Comercio. "Las instalaciones del hotel Hilton Colón fueron atacadas en Quito" October 8, 2019: https://www.elcomercio.com/actualidad/ataque-hotel-hilton-colon-quito.html (accessed April 4, 2020).

El Comercio. "Petroecuador declara Fuerza Mayor sobre todas sus operaciones de venta de crudo" October 9, 2019: https://www.elcomercio.com/actualidad/petroecuador-fuerza-mayor-venta-crudo.html (accessed April 4, 2020).

El Comercio. "Defensoría del Pueblo confirma la muerte de un dirigente indígena en Quito" October 10, 2019: https://www.elcomercio.com/actualidad/defensoria-muerte-manifestante-conaie-protestas.html (accessed April 4, 2020).

El Comercio. "91 vías cerradas, violencia y quemas paralizaron a Quito este sábado 12 de octubre del 2019" October 13, 2019: https://www.elcomercio.com/actualidad/cierres-vias-quito-violencia-quemas.html (accessed April 4, 2020).

El Telégrafo. "El bloque 61 se beneficia con una alianza público-privada" December 16, 2015: https://www.eltelegrafo.com.ec/noticias/economia/8/el-bloque-61-se-beneficia-con-una-alianza-publico-privada (accessed July 15, 2019).

El Universo. "Auca se explotará con francesa Schlumberger" December 16, 2015: https://www.eluniverso.com/noticias/2015/12/16/nota/5300823/auca-se-explotara-francesa-schlumberger (accessed July 15, 2019).

Escobar, Arturo. "Beyond the third world: Imperial globality, global coloniality and anti-globalisation social movements" *Third World Quarterly* 25:1 (2004) 207–230.

Escobar, Arturo. *Designs for the Pluriverse: Radical Interdependence, Autonomy and the Making of Worlds*. Durham: Duke University Press, 2018.

Fanon, Frantz. *The Wretched of the Earth*. New York: Grove Press, 2004.

Ferrell, Jeff. "Criminological Verstehen: Inside the immediacy of crime" in *Ethnography at the Edge: Crime, Deviance and Field Research*, edited by Jeff Ferrell and Mark Hamm (20–42). Boston: Northeastern University Press, 1998.

Ferrell, Jeff and Mark Hamm. *Ethnography at the Edge: Crime, Deviance and Field Research* Boston: Northeastern University Press, 1998.

Financial Times. "Schlumberger cuts 10,000 jobs amid oil price rout" January 22, 2016: https://www.ft.com/content/1127279a-c08b-11e5-846f-79b0e3d20eaf (accessed July 15, 2019).

Fontaine, Guillaume. *Los conflictos ambientales por petróleo y la crisis de gobernanza ambiental en el Ecuador*. Madrid: Centro de Investigación para la Paz, 2009.

Fun-Sang, B. et al. "Restoring the Auca field potential through formation damage removal" paper presented at the SPE International Conference and Exhibition on Formation Damage Control, Lafayette, 7–9 February 2018.

Galarza Zavala, Jaime. *El festín del petróleo*. Quito: Sur Editores, 2012.

Gómez-Barris, Macarena. *The Extractive Zone: Social Ecologies and Decolonial Perspectives*. Durham: Duke University Press, 2017.

Graeber, David. "Radical alterity is just another way of saying "reality": A reply to Eduardo Viveiros de Castro" *Hau: Journal of Ethnographic Theory* 5:2 (2015) 1–41.

Grosfoguel, Ramon. "The epistemic decolonial turn" *Cultural Studies* 21:2–3 (2007) 211–223.

Gudynas, Eduardo. "Extractivisms: Tendencies and consequences" in *Reframing Latin American Development* edited by Ronaldo Munck and Raúl Delgado Wise (61–76). Abingdon: Routledge, 2018.

Haider, Asad. *Mistaken Identity: Race and Class in the Age of Trump*. New York: Verso, 2018.

Hecht, Susanna and Alexander Cockburn. *The Fate of the Forest: Developers, Destroyers, and Defenders of the Amazon*. London: Penguin, 1990.

Holquist, Michael. "Prologue" in *Rabelais and His World*, edited by Mikhail Bakhtin (xiii–xxiii). Bloomington: Indiana University Press, 1984.

James, C.L.R. *The Black Jacobins: Toussaint L'ouverture and the San Domingo Revolution*. London: Penguin, 2001.

Kapoor, Ilan and Zahi Zalloua. *Universal Politics*. Oxford: Oxford University Press, 2021.

Kimerling, Judith S. *Amazon Crude*. New York: Natural Resources Defense Council, 1991.

Kothari, Ashish, Ariel Salleh, Arturo Escobar, Federico Demaria and Alberto Acosta. "Introduction: Finding pluriversal paths" in *Pluriverse: A Post-Development Dictionary*, edited by Ashish Kothari et al. (xii–xl) New Delhi: Tulika, 2019.

La Hora. "Campo Auca: El mecanismo de pago es un secreto" March 15, 2016: https://lahora.com.ec/noticia/1101925283/campo-auca-el-mecanismo-de-pago-es-un-secretoplatform=hootsuite (accessed July 15, 2019).

Labban, Mazen. "Against shareholder value: Accumulation in the oil industry and the biopolitics of labour under finance" *Antipode* 46:2 (2014) 477–496.

Larrea, Carlos. "Extractivism, economic diversification and prospects for sustainable development in Ecuador" paper presented at the conference "Latin America and the Shifting Sands of Global Power", Australia National University, Canberra, September 11–12, 2013.

Linebaugh, Peter and Marcus Rediker. *The Many-Headed Hydra: The Hidden History of the Revolutionary Atlantic*. London: Verso, 2012.

Llori, Guadalupe. "Carta abierta a todas las embajadas, consulados, organizaciones defensoras de los derechos humanos, medios de comunicación" Oficio Circular no. 292-HCPO-P, 7 April, 2007 (personal archives of Dositeo Cuenca).

Lu, Flora, Gabriela Valdivia and Nestor Silva. *Oil, Revolution and Indigenous Citizenship in Ecuadorian Amazonia*. New York: Palgrave Macmillan, 2017.

Mader, Elke. *Metamorfosis del poder: Persona, mito y visión en la sociedad de Shuar y Achuar (Ecuador, Perú)*. Quito: Abya Yala, 1999.

Martínez, Javier. *El paraíso en venta: desarrollo, etnicidad y ambientalismo en la frontera de Yasuní (Amazonia ecuatoriana)*. Quito: Abya Yala, 2015.

McGowan, Todd. *Universality and Identity Politics*. New York: Columbia University Press, 2020.

Mignolo, Walter. "The geopolitics of knowledge and the colonial difference" *The South Atlantic Quarterly* 10:1 (2002) 57–96.

Mignolo, Walter. "Geopolitics of sensing and knowing: On (de)coloniality, border thinking and epistemic disobedience" *Postcolonial Studies* 14:3 (2011) 273–283.

Moore, Jason W. *Capitalism in the Web of Life: Ecology and the Accumulation of Capital*. London: Verso, 2015.

MPD Sucumbíos. *Las valerosas jornadas de los pueblos del Nororiente*. Ecuatoriano Lago Agrio: Ediciones Opción, 2006.

Nasdaq. "Schlumberger's operations in Ecuador face financial crunch" November 16, 2017: https://www.nasdaq.com/articles/schlumbergers-operations-ecuador-face-financial-crunch-2017-11-16 (accessed November 21, 2019).

Oil Price. "'the worst is behind us': Schlumberger CEO sees reasons for optimism" July 22, 2016: https://oilprice.com/Energy/Energy-General/The-Worst-Is-Behind-Us-Schlumberger-CEO-Sees-Reason-For-Optimism.html (accessed July 15, 2019).

Ortiz, Pablo. "Protestas locales amazónicas y modelo petrolero en Ecuador" *OSAL* 17 (2005) 53–60.

Ospina, Pablo. "La orden de prisión a Rafael Correa y las denuncias de corrupción" *La Línea de Fuego* July 10, 2018: https://lalineadefuego.info/2018/07/10/la-orden-de-prision-a-rafael-correa-y-las-denuncias-de-corrupcion-por-pablo-ospina-peralta/ (accessed December 16, 2018).

Pellizaro, Siro. *Mitología Shuar volumen 10: Shakaim, mitos de la selva y del desmonte*. Quito: Abya Yala, 1988.

Petroamazonas. "Informe técnico, económico y legal de negociación" *Memorando N0. PAM-LGL-2015-00148*, December 11, 2015 (internal company document).

Pichon, Francisco. "Colonist land-allocation decisions, land use and deforestation in the Ecuadorian amazon frontier" *Economic Development and Cultural Change* 45:4 (1997) 707–744.

Primacías. "Paro afecta el 37% de la producción de crudo de Petroamazonas" October 8, 2019: https://www.primicias.ec/noticias/economia/paro-afecta-37-produccion-crudo-petroamazonas/ (accessed April 4, 2020).

Purcell, Thomas F. and Estefanía Martínez. "Post-neoliberal energy modernity and the political economy of the landlord state in Ecuador" *Energy Research and Social Science* 41 (2018) 12–21.

Restrepo, Marco. "El proceso de acumulación en la Amazonia ecuatoriana: una breve visión histórica" in *Amazonia nuestra: una visión alternativa*, edited by Lucy Ruiz (105–124). Quito: Abya Yala, 1991.

Reuters. "Ecuador to sign payment deal for Schlumberger debt" November 16, 2017: https://www.reuters.com/article/us-ecuador-oil/ecuador-to-sign-payment-deal-for-schlumberger-debt-idUSKBN1DG07K (accessed November 21, 2019).

Rig Zone. "Schlumberger cuts 2,000 more jobs in full-scale industry crisis" April 21, 2016: https://www.rigzone.com/news/oil_gas/a/144142/schlumberger_cuts_2000_more_jobs_in_fullscale_industry_crisis/ (accessed July 15, 2019).

Riofrancos, Thea. *Resource Radicals: From Petro-Nationalism to Post-Extractivism in Ecuador*. Durham: Duke University Press, 2020.

Rival, Laura. *Huaorani Transformations in Twenty-First Century Ecuador: Treks into the Future of Time*. Tucson: University of Arizona Press, 2016.

Rivas, Teresa. "Schlumberger: The slump will continue" *Barron's*, October 11, 2017: https://www.barrons.com/articles/schlumberger-the-slump-will-continue-1507732039 (accessed November 21, 2019).

Rivera Cusicanqui, Silvia. "Ch'ixinakax Utxiwa: A reflection on the practices and discourses of decolonization" *The South Atlantic Quarterly* 111:1 (2012) 95–109.

Santillana, Alejandra. "Protestas en Ecuador: del paro que no paró hasta devolvernos la esperanza" *La Linea de Fuego*, November 6, 2019: https://lalineadefuego.info/2019/11/06/protestas-en-ecuador-del-paro-que-no-paro-hasta-devolvernos-la-esperanza/ (accessed April 4, 2020).

Santos, Mariano. "El entreguismo petrolero" *Revista Rupturas*, 2016: http://www.revistarupturas.com/el-entreguismo-petrolero.html (accessed July 15, 2019).

Sawyer, Suzana. *Crude Chronicles: Indigenous Politics, Multinational Oil and Neoliberalism in Ecuador*. Durham: Duke University Press, 2004.

Schaefer, Timo. "Engaging modernity: The political making of indigenous movements in Bolivia and Ecuador (1900-2008)" *Third World Quarterly* 30:2 (2009) 397–413.

Sigcha, Amparo. "Sucumbíos y Orellana: Un paro que se enfrentó al imperialismo" *Red Voltaire*, September 1, 2005: http://www.voltairenet.org/article127239.html (accessed September 22, 2017).

Svampa, Maristella. *Neo-extractivism in Latin America: Socio-Environmental Conflicts, the Territorial Turn, and New Political Narratives*. Cambridge: Cambridge University Press, 2019.

Swyngedouw, Erik. *Promises of the Political: Insurgent Cities in a Post-Political Environment*. Cambridge: MIT Press, 2018.

Techint. *The Techint Group 2017*. Techint: Buenos Aires, 2018.

Thompson, Hunter S. *Hell's Angels: A Strange and Terrible Saga* London: Penguin, 2003.

Thompson, Hunter S. *Fear and Loathing in Las Vegas: A Savage Journey to the Heart of the American Dream*. London: Harper Perennial, 2005.

Thompson, Hunter S. *Fear and Loathing on the Campaign Trail '72*. London: Harper Perennial, 2005.

Thompson, Hunter S. *Happy Birthday, Jack Nicholson*. London: Penguin, 2005.

Thompson, Hunter S. *The Gonzo Papers Anthology*. Basingstoke, Picador, 2009.

Tomba, Massimiliano. *Insurgent Universality: An Alternative Legacy of Modernity*. New York: Oxford University Press, 2019.

Tsing, Anna. *Friction: An Ethnography of Global Connection*. Princeton: Princeton University Press, 2005.

Valdivia, Gabriela. "Jugarse La Vida: Urban political ecologies of oil and marronage" *Antipode* 53:6 (2021) 1829–1852.

Veltmeyer, Henry. "Resistance, class struggle and social movements in Latin America: Contemporary dynamics" *Journal of Peasant Studies* 46:6 (2019) 1264–1285.

Villavicencio, Fernando. "Exclusivo: contrato Campo Auca, loteria para Schlumberger, migajas para Ecuador" *Focus Ecuador* June 8, 2017: https://medium.com/focus-news-ecuador/exclusivo-contrato-campo-auca-lotería-para-schlumberger-migajas-para-ecuador-c6bdea18e9c6 (accessed July 15, 2019).

Villavicencio, Fernando. "Otra más de Correa y Glas: Contraloria detecta irregularidades de entrega del Campo Auca" *Focus Ecuador*, October 21, 2017: https://medium.com/focus-news-ecuador/otra-más-de-correa-y-glas-contraloría-detecta-irregularidades-de-entrega-del-campo-auca-1cf64769f923 (accessed July 15, 2019.)

Viteri Toro, Jorge A. Petróleo. *lanzas y sangre*. Quito: La Palabra, 2008.

Walsh, Catherine. "'Other' knowledges, 'other' critiques: Reflections on the politics and practices of philosophy and decoloniality in the 'other' America" *Transmodernity* 1:3 (2012) 11–27.

Watts, Michael. "Petro-violence: Community, extraction, and political ecology of a mythic commodity" in *Violent Environments*, edited by Nancy Lee Peluso and Michael Watts (189–212). Ithaca: Cornell University Press, 2001.

Watts, Michael. "Accumulating insecurity and manufacturing risk along the energy frontier" in *Risking Capitalism*, edited by Susan Soederberg (197–236). Bingley: Emerald, 2016.

Wesche, Rolf. "Ecotourism and indigenous peoples in the resource frontier of the Ecuadorian Amazon" *Yearbook, Conference of Latin Americanist Geographers*, 19 (1993) 35–45.

Wilson, Japhy. *Reality of Dreams: Post-Neoliberal Utopias in the Ecuadorian Amazon*. New Haven: Yale University Press, 2021.

Wilson, Japhy. "The insurgent universal: Between Eurocentric universalism and the pluriverse" *Nordia Geographical Publications* 51:2 (2022) 153–162.

Wilson, Japhy and Manuel Bayón. *La selva de los elefantes blancos: megaproyectos y extractivismos en la Amazonía ecuatoriana*. Quito: Abya Yala, 2017.

Winston, Matthew, *Gonzo Text: Disentangling Meaning in Hunter S. Thompson's Journalism*. New York: Peter Lang, 2014.

Wright, Greg. "The literary, political and legal strategies of Oscar Zeta Acosta and Hunter S. Thompson: Intertextuality, ambiguity, and (naturally) fear and loathing" *The Journal of Popular Culture* 43:3 (2010) 622–643.

Ye, Jingzhong, Jan Douwe van der Ploeg, Sergio Schneider and Teodor Shanin. "The incursions of extractivism: Moving from dispersed places to global capitalism" *Journal of Peasant Studies* 47:1 (2019) 155–183.

Žižek, Slavoj. *The Ticklish Subject: The Absent Centre of Political Ontology*. New York: Verso, 1999.

Žižek, Slavoj. *In Defense of Lost Causes*. New York: Verso, 2008.

Index

For Product Safety Concerns and Information please contact our EU representative GPSR@taylorandfrancis.com Taylor & Francis Verlag GmbH, Kaufingerstraße 24, 80331 München, Germany